Edited by
Giampaolo Bianconi
and Caitlin Haskell

With contributions by
Giampaolo Bianconi,
Caitlin Haskell,
Hannah B Higgins,
Jacqueline Humphries,
and Jack Shear

Ellsworth Kelly: Spectrum
Colors Arranged by Chance

The Art Institute of Chicago
Distributed by Yale University Press,
New Haven and London

Contents

FOREWORD

Ellsworth Kelly lived and worked in Paris for six years after serving in World War II, from 1948 to 1954, during which time he explored, experimented, and honed his artistic vision. Over the course of two months in 1951, Kelly produced a series of eight large-scale collages, known as *Spectrum Colors Arranged by Chance*, that would prove to be pivotal to his artistic practice. This publication commemorates an exhibition at the Art Institute of Chicago that brought these eight collages together for the first time, along with a ninth and final collage and a related painting, both made in 1953.

To make each *Spectrum Colors* collage, Kelly meticulously cut squares out of *papier gommette*, a gum-backed colored paper commonly used by French schoolchildren, then arranged the squares on a grid using a chance-based process. The eighteen available colors of *papier gommette* allowed for virtually limitless combinations, enabling Kelly to work freely. The sequence of the collages reflects the progression of his careful experiments with chance and the interplay of white, black, and color. Kelly's breakthrough was inspired in part by earlier abstract artists who used chance to determine certain elements of their compositions, as well as a collective rejection of traditional modes of painting. In a letter he wrote to John Cage in 1950 during this transformative moment in Paris, Kelly described a conceit of painting that would guide his work for nearly seven decades: "My collages are only ideas for things much larger—things to cover walls. In fact all the things I've done I would like to see much larger. I am not interested in painting as it has been accepted for so long—to hang on the walls of houses as pictures. To hell with pictures— they should *be* the wall—even better—on the outside wall— of large buildings."

The concept Kelly conveyed to Cage later materialized in monochromatic panels designed to interact within architectural settings. In 1999 the Art Institute commissioned Kelly to create a series of six new acrylic paintings on sculptural fiberglass panels for permanent display in the upper courtyard of the Daniel F. and Ada L. Rice Building. As a curator at the time, I had the distinct privilege of working with the artist during his many trips to the Art Institute to oversee the planning and installation of these now iconic *Chicago Panels*. Their installation coincided with the opening of the groundbreaking exhibition *Ellsworth Kelly: The Early Drawings, 1948–1955* in the Rice galleries, which featured three of the

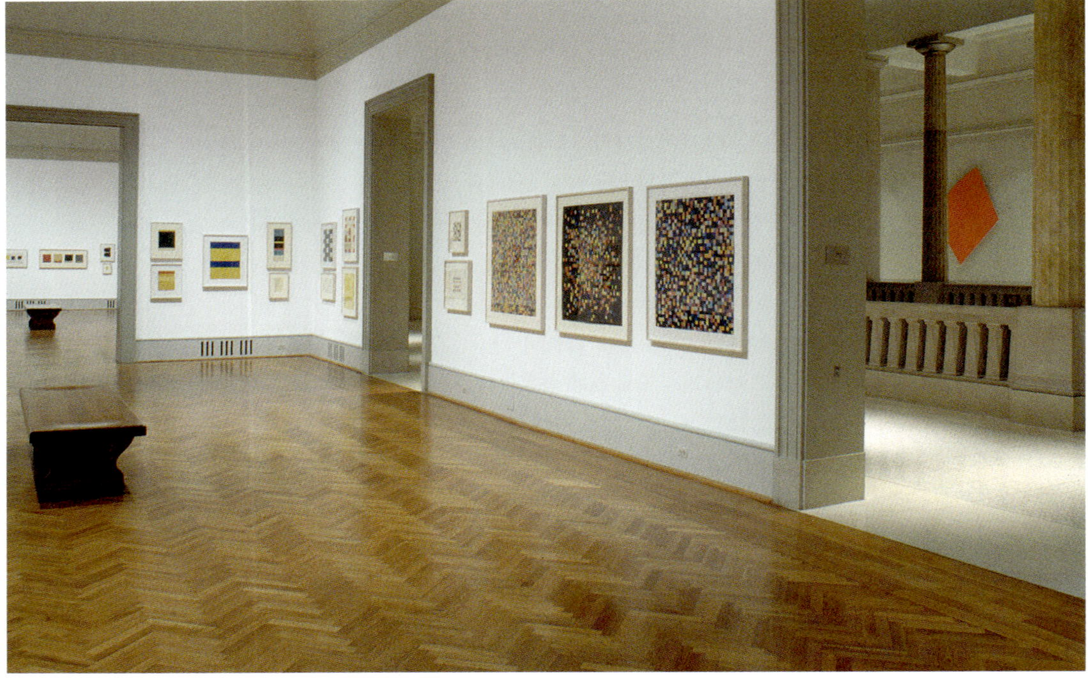

Fig. 1. Installation view of the exhibition *Ellsworth Kelly: The Early Drawings, 1948–1955*, the Art Institute of Chicago, September 11–December 5, 1999, featuring (from right) Ellsworth Kelly's *Spectrum Colors Arranged by Chance VI, Spectrum Colors Arranged by Chance IV*, and *Spectrum Colors Arranged by Chance VII*. Visible through the doorway at right is the upper level of the courtyard of the Daniel F. and Ada L. Rice Building with one of the newly commissioned *Chicago Panels* (1989–99).

Spectrum Colors Arranged by Chance collages. This installation of more than two hundred of Kelly's early works was separated by forty years of artistic exploration from the *Chicago Panels*, yet the adjacent displays revealed the continuity of Kelly's instinctive visual vocabulary. Rooted in color, form, and shape, Kelly's artistic endeavor had evolved and found its apex in what he described as "a closer contact between the artist and the wall, and a new spirit of art accompanying contemporary architecture" (see fig. 1).

The Art Institute is proud of its long-standing commitment to Kelly's work and vision. Thanks to the extraordinary generosity of Jack Shear and the Ellsworth Kelly Studio, the museum now holds two works from the storied *Spectrum Colors* series in our permanent collection: *Spectrum Colors Arranged by Chance IV* (pp. 54–55) and the final collage, *Spectrum Colors Arranged by Chance IX* (pp. 64–65), gifted on the occasion of this exhibition. These collages join other early works on paper, multipart canvases (*Train Landscape* [see fig. 4] and *Red Yellow Blue White and Black II*), monochrome paintings (*Tableau Vert*), and shaped canvases (*Chatham XII: Yellow Black*) that collectively chart Kelly's rigorous pursuit to clarify the relationship of color, form, and shape. This career-long set of commitments is evident in the *Chicago Panels* and *White Curve*, another permanent monumental installation at the Art Institute that merges art and architecture, defining the experience of the museum's Pritzker Garden for visitors.

The exhibition of the complete *Spectrum Colors Arranged by Chance* series became the impetus for Art Institute co-curators Caitlin Haskell, Gary C. and Frances Comer Senior Curator, Modern and Contemporary Art, and Director, Ray Johnson Collections and Research; and Giampaolo Bianconi, Dittmer Associate Curator, Modern and Contemporary Art, to host a compelling conversation with art historian Hannah B Higgins, artist Jacqueline Humphries, and Jack Shear, Kelly's husband and president of the Ellsworth Kelly Foundation. I am grateful to each of them for bringing their insights and fresh perspectives to consider the series anew, both holistically and contextually.

By spotlighting this important early body of work, the exhibition, together with the discussion it inspired, and this publication shed light on a critical chapter in the career of one of the defining artists of the past century.

James Rondeau, President and Eloise W. Martin Director, The Art Institute of Chicago

ACKNOWLEDGMENTS

During the festivities of the Ellsworth Kelly Centennial in 2023, the Art Institute of Chicago recognized a surprising gap in the artist's formidable exhibition history. One of Kelly's most formative bodies of work from his early years in France—the nine large-scale collages and the painting known as *Spectrum Colors Arranged by Chance*—had never before been presented in its entirety. A quick consultation of the literature on Kelly confirmed this lacuna, and we began to hope that, with the support of Jack Shear and the Ellsworth Kelly Studio, as well as the collaboration of several esteemed museums and private collections, it might be possible to bring these works together. The prospect of exhibiting the series in its entirety for the first time was thrilling to us, and happily this ambition struck a chord with other admirers of Kelly's work as a fitting way to mark the close of his centennial tributes.

Foremost thanks are due to James Rondeau, President and Eloise W. Martin Director of the Art Institute, for his vision in pursuing this extraordinary opportunity and for entrusting us with the presentation and publication of the *Spectrum Colors* series. Sarah Guernsey, both during her time as Interim Chair, Modern and Contemporary Art, and as always, as Deputy Director and Senior Vice President for Curatorial Affairs, provided essential guidance at every stage. The support of Sarah Kelly Oehler, Vice President of Curatorial Strategy and Field-McCormick Chair and Curator, Arts of the Americas; David Nacol, Senior Vice President, Philanthropy; Katie Rahn, Senior Vice President, Marketing and Communications; Emily Benedict, Vice President, Campus Operations; Amy Allen, Vice President, Engagement; and Aaron Anderson, Associate Vice President, Financial Planning and Analysis, was equally crucial.

At the Ellsworth Kelly Studio, Jack Shear, Mary Anne Lee, Allison Wucher, and the entirety of the dedicated staff made every aspect of this project possible and all their resources readily accessible. Thanks to their extraordinary generosity, the ninth and final collage in the *Spectrum Colors* series, which was loaned to the exhibition by the Ellsworth Kelly Studio, has now become a part of the permanent collection of the Art Institute, for which we are extremely grateful.

Realizing this project as part of Kelly's centennial relied on the swift assembly of each work in the *Spectrum Colors* series, and for this we are thankful for the responsiveness, professionalism, and collaboration of each of our lenders: Steven Cohen; Jack Shear and Mary Anne Lee, Ellsworth Kelly Studio, Spencertown, New York; Laura Satersmoen, Fisher Art Foundation, San Francisco; Aaron I. Fleischman and Lin Lougheed; Emily Wei Rales, Glenstone, Potomac, Maryland; Marie-Josée and Henry R. Kravis; Glenn Lowry, Christophe Cherix, Jodi Hauptman, and River Bullock, Museum of Modern Art, New York; Sasha Suda and Louis Marchesano, Philadelphia Museum of Art; Christopher Bedford and Janet Bishop, San Francisco Museum of Modern Art; Charles and Helen Schwab; and Mary Zlot. At the Art Institute, Mark Pascale, Kevin Salatino, and Emily Ziemba in Prints and Drawings and Mardy Sears,

Senior Conservation Technician, Paper, were essential to organizing the interdepartmental loan of work from the museum's collection, as well as sharing their knowledge on all things Ellsworth Kelly.

We are deeply grateful to the participants in our round-table conversation: Hannah B Higgins, Professor of Intermedia and Avant-Garde Art and Culture at the University of Illinois Chicago, whose perspective helped to shape our conversation and provided solid ground for its foundations; Jacqueline Humphries, artist and incisive dialogue partner; and Jack Shear, for his willingness to share his singular expertise. As we were preparing the exhibition, Yve-Alain Bois, author of the catalogue raisonné of Kelly's paintings, reliefs, and sculpture, lent his perceptive eye to our exhibition text.

Joining us in this curatorial endeavor at the Art Institute, Tamar Kharatishvili, Alivé Piliado Santana, and Tacy Wagner helped to realize this exhibition and publication at different stages of their development. Kate Tierney Powell in the office of the President and Director provided key institutional context for Kelly's works in the Art Institute. Briana Gonzalez managed the exhibition with grace and efficiency. She was joined by Ariana Weber, who capably oversaw the loans. Nicholas Barron and Christina Warzecha provided sensitive observation and movement of the artworks. In Conservation, Sylvie Pénichon and Gillian Marcus ensured each work was cared for at every stage. Ginia Sweeney and Sheila Majumdar thoughtfully edited the exhibition text. In Modern and Contemporary Art, our colleagues Paulina Pobocha, Makayla May, Jay Dandy, Annika Bohanec, and Joanna Abijaoude must be thanked, for without them nothing inside or outside of this book could have been realized.

Our colleagues in Publishing—Katie Reilly, with Lauren Makholm, Lisa Meyerowitz, Ben Bertin, David Khan-Giordano, and Isella Sandoval—shepherded this book from its inception to completion. Sarah Noreika expertly edited the texts. Ken Meier of Common Name designed this book with creativity and a sensitive understanding of its mission. In Imaging, under the leadership of Bonnie Rosenberg, Nathan Keay, Robert Lifson, Jonathan Mathias, and Juan Molina Hernández provided outstanding photography. Kaitlyn Fultz-Campion and Hayley Hinsberger worked postproduction magic, and Elyse M. Allen led the Production team.

Our deepest appreciation, however, is due to Ellsworth Kelly, whose visionary body of work and historic ties to the Art Institute of Chicago continue to generate new ways of seeing and understanding the art of the past and present, and to Jack Shear, for his tireless commitment to ensuring that Kelly's work remains as relevant and vibrant today as it was seventy years ago.

Caitlin Haskell, Gary C. and Frances Comer Senior Curator, Modern and Contemporary Art, and Director, Ray Johnson Collections and Research

Giampaolo Bianconi, Dittmer Associate Curator, Modern and Contemporary Art

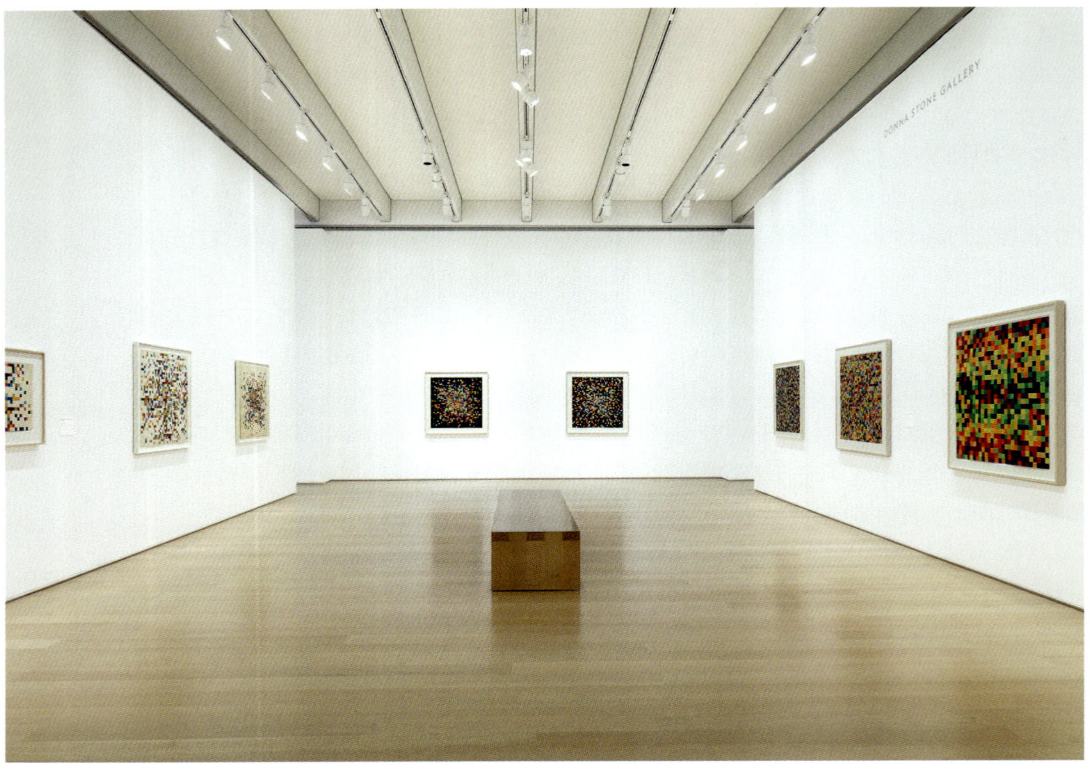

Fig. 2.   Installation view of the exhibition *Ellsworth Kelly: Spectrum Colors Arranged by Chance*, the Art Institute of Chicago, June 22–September 9, 2024.

Introduction: New Perspectives on Ellsworth Kelly's *Spectrum Colors Arranged by Chance*

Caitlin Haskell

Introduction

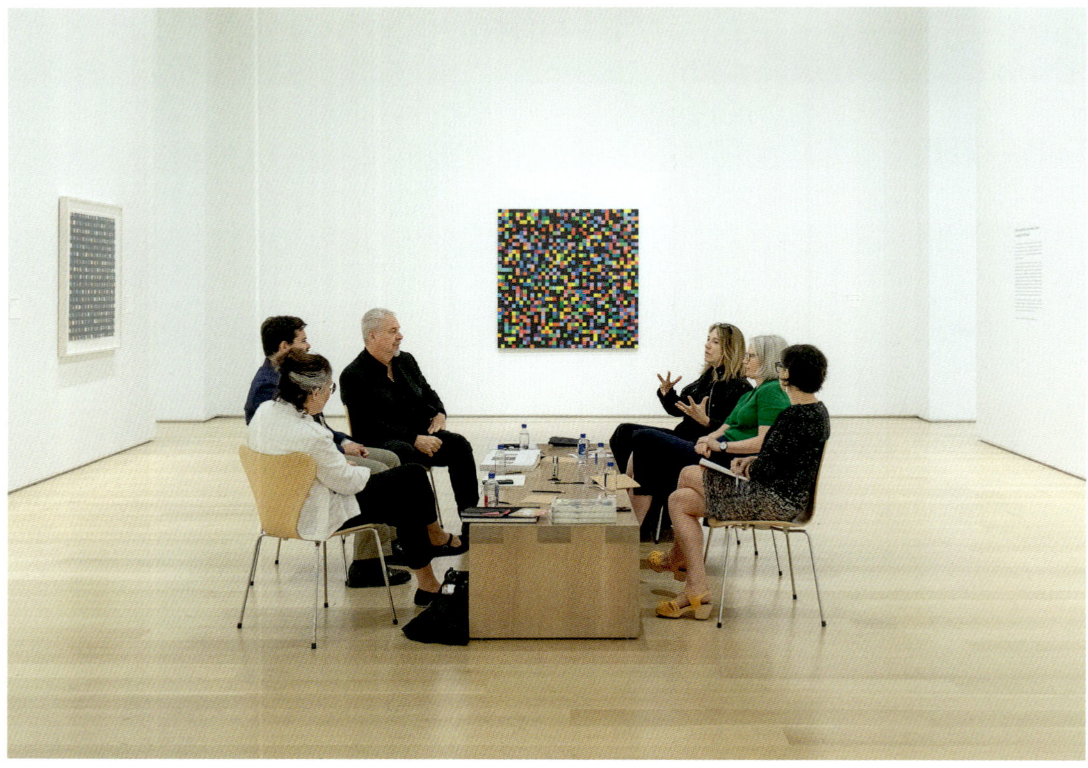

Fig. 3.   Roundtable on Ellsworth Kelly's *Spectrum Colors Arranged by Chance*,
the Art Institute of Chicago, July 10, 2024, with (clockwise from left)
Hannah B Higgins, Giampaolo Bianconi, Jack Shear, Jacqueline Humphries,
Caitlin Haskell, and Katie Reilly.

Ellsworth Kelly belonged to the cohort of American artists who felt a strong pull toward Paris in the years after World War II and an equally strong urge to return to the United States in the 1950s, reentering the New York art world during the years of Abstract Expressionism's predominance. The extraordinary works that Kelly produced in France, between 1948 and 1954, are rightly regarded as foundational to his oeuvre. A wellspring of ideas that served the artist for decades, these works have also been a Rosetta stone for scholars, allowing historians to interpret Kelly's work with unusual coherence across the full span of his career. Even so, Kelly's early production in France has experienced a double dislocation of sorts, geographically separate from the activity of his generational peers and critically belated, finding reception in American artistic discourse only in the 1960s. The extent to which Kelly's early works connect to previous generations of European Modernism or to later Minimal art was, and remains, a perennial topic of interest. What has been harder to perceive is the works' relationship to the moment of their creation. Indeed, when critical thought finally caught up with Kelly's astoundingly prescient practice, the geographical and chronological dislocation of his early works meant that they continued to await evaluation on their own terms—that is, as pioneering new forms developed within the nascent plurality now recognized as a hallmark of the 1950s.

The roundtable discussion presented herein, convened on July 10, 2024, at the Art Institute of Chicago, addresses the dislocations of Kelly's early work, as well as the continuities among these works and expanded historical understandings of midcentury practices that are freshly perceptible today. At the center of the conversation is *Spectrum Colors Arranged by Chance*, a group of nine large-scale collages and one painting produced in France between 1951 and 1953. From June 22 to September 9, 2024, the full series was presented to the public for the first time, displayed in a dedicated gallery within the Art Institute's Modern and Contemporary collection galleries.[1] In this context, the *Spectrum Colors* series was arranged sequentially, allowing viewers to experience Kelly's progression through the series in a way that, to date, had not been possible. Moreover, the series was placed in proximity and with occasional sight lines to contemporaneous works by Karel Appel (1951), Lygia Clark (1958), Willem de Kooning (1948/49 and 1950), Helen Frankenthaler (1952), Barbara Hepworth (1954–55), Joan Mitchell (1955), Barnett Newman (1946 and 1950), Jackson Pollock (1953), and Kelly (1953) himself,

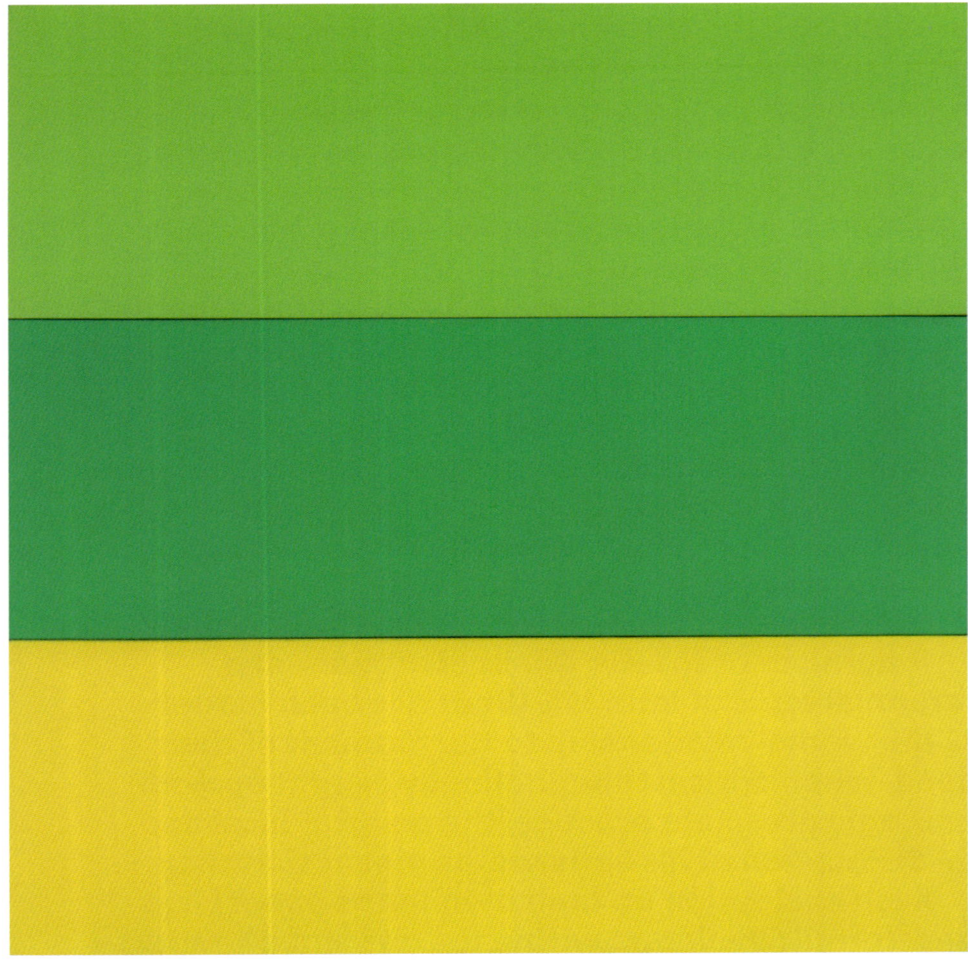

Fig. 4.   Ellsworth Kelly (American, 1923–2015). *Train Landscape*, 1953.
Oil on canvas; 3 joined panels; 111.8 × 111.8 cm (44 × 44 in.). The Art Institute
of Chicago, gift of the Ellsworth Kelly Foundation and Jack Shear, 2025.108.

with works by contemporaries such as Robert Rauschenberg
and Cy Twombly in neighboring spaces. These adjacent
works were on display independently from the intervention
of *Spectrum Colors Arranged by Chance*, yet I mention them
to prepare the reader for a significant undercurrent within the
roundtable discussion: Where once this moment in the early
1950s was primarily oriented toward Abstract Expressionism,
a thoughtful assessment of this stage of Kelly's career must
now take into account germinal forms of experimental
practices such as Fluxus, new media, and Minimal art, as
well as a range of complementary and attitudinally aligned
engagements with contemporary painting in Europe.

Joining Giampaolo Bianconi and myself for the roundtable
were Hannah B Higgins, Jacqueline Humphries, and Jack
Shear. The five of us represent the concerns and priorities
of creative practice, curatorial work, and the writing of art
history, yet the reader will see that each participant spoke
from personal experience in ways that cross strict professional
delineations. Each of us allowed the works—and the occasion
to see the series together as an ensemble—to be our guides.
Our conversation was also influenced by the work of the
scholars who have published on the collages most cogently,
and in this regard Yve-Alain Bois merits individual attention.
Bois's work not only has allowed us to grasp the conditions
of the making of *Spectrum Colors Arranged by Chance*—the
motivations that led to the works' production and informed
their specific material and visual qualities—but also has charted
the history of their reception, a circuitous path of fits and starts
with numerous misreadings along the way.[2] He has argued
persuasively that we would do well to avoid tying the works
too closely to that of abstract artists active in Europe prior to
World War II—for example, Piet Mondrian, Ben Nicholson, and
Georges Vantongerloo. He also has helped to bring the works
out from the shadow cast on them by the tendency of scholars
to understand *Spectrum Colors Arranged by Chance* as a kind
of precursor to Minimal art achieved precociously in the 1950s
by a stroke of luck. Indeed, it is true that Kelly was a beneficiary,
in some senses, to the critical vocabulary that became available
with Minimal art and that enabled a new measure of analytical
specificity in addressing works such as the *Spectrum Colors*
series. However, like so many artworks deemed stylistically
"proto," interpreting these collages and painting requires
that we take special care to neither over-determine nor under-
acknowledge the knowingness of Kelly's achievement.

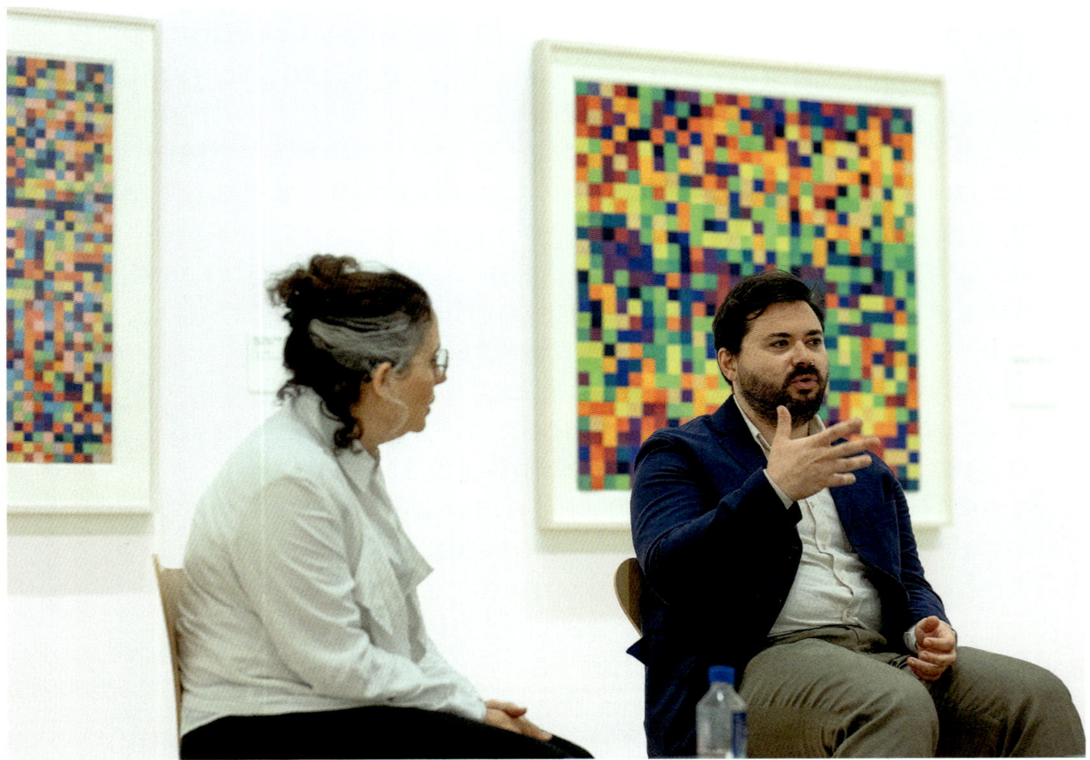

Fig. 5.   Roundtable on Ellsworth Kelly's *Spectrum Colors Arranged by Chance*, the Art Institute of Chicago, July 10, 2024.

Building upon what we know of the origins and objectives of *Spectrum Colors Arranged by Chance*, the roundtable engaged with the question at the heart of our exhibition: What do we see when the collages are viewed together today? In the presence of the reassembled series, one becomes immediately attuned to the works' impressive ambition in terms of both their size and their increasing complexity across ten iterations. Equally plain is the great versatility of these works, their modularity lending itself to endless new explorations of color combinations and variously scaled formats. During the roundtable, Shear drew attention to the providential nature of the collages, whose pathbreaking effects transcend their humble materials. Created at a time when Kelly had only the barest financial resources, the collages and painting could easily have been lost to history had Kelly not managed to self-fund their return with him to the United States. Shear's unparalleled perspective on Kelly's working process allowed us to attend with precision to the collage's iterative logic, progressing as a succession of problems posed and solved in which a solution need not imply finality. He also spoke to the material history of the works and their ties to the body, looking for marks of Kelly's hand in the preparatory gridding of the collages' paper supports and reminding us of the practicalities of working with *papier gommette* (gum-backed construction paper), a material made sticky by the application of an aqueous solution Kelly always had at hand—his own saliva.

Critical and art historical interest in *Spectrum Colors Arranged by Chance* has tended to focus on Kelly's use of "ready-made" color and his engagement with non-compositional strategies (discussed at length within). *Papier gommette*, as has often been noted, had the double advantage of offering a predetermined set of colors and a way of putting down color without a brush. However, as Higgins observed, even within the twentieth-century legacy of chance, it is possible to take a more expansive view of the series. For example, the resonance of chance in the work of Jean (Hans) Arp, whom Kelly visited in France in February 1950, shortly before making the *Spectrum Colors* collages, may be overstated when regarded in isolation. Has enthusiasm for the historical certainty of that visit prevented us from seeing connections to chance elsewhere?

Similarly, viewing the full series provides an opportunity to reexamine Kelly's pursuit of authorial anonymity as an essential feature of the works. Kelly's removal of subjectivity was on the level of mark (an insistence that no habits of the

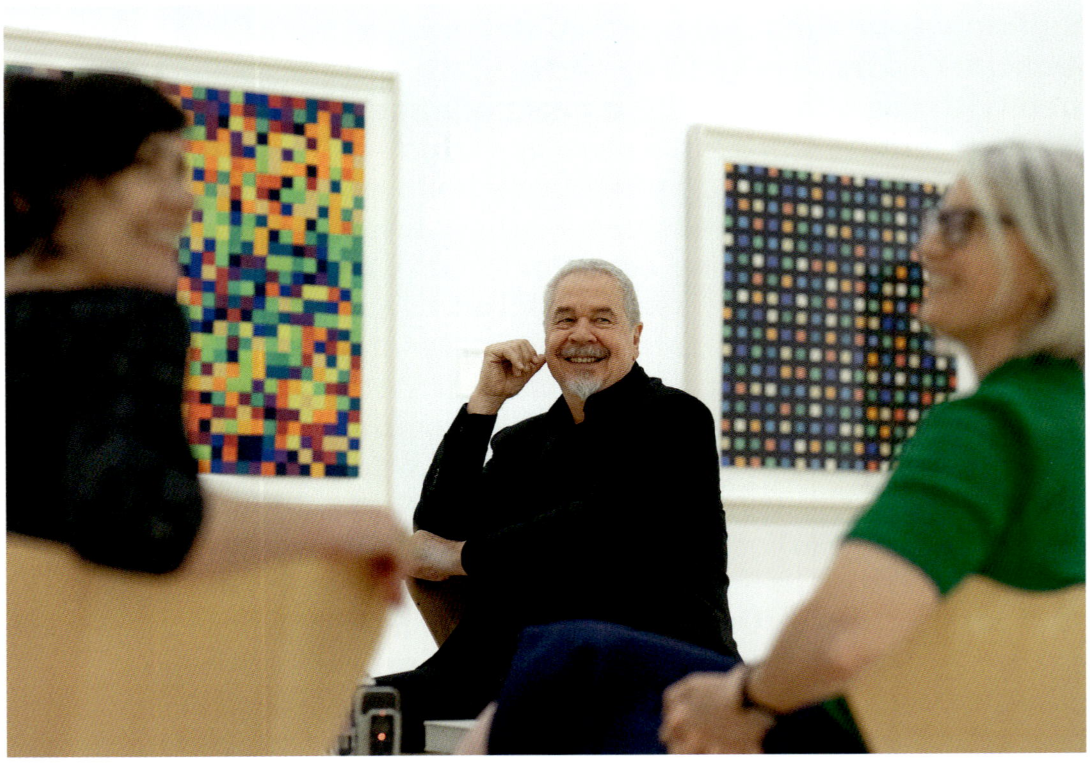

Fig. 6.   Roundtable on Ellsworth Kelly's *Spectrum Colors Arranged by Chance*, the Art Institute of Chicago, July 10, 2024.

artist's hand would be evident), and it extended to the removal of style and composition through his use of random processes and an organizing grid in which uniform shapes of color were laid down. Yet the removal of the artist's choice and the rigid structure of the grid do not diminish the animating, at times unruly force of the color itself. Humphries helped us to see the grid as the slippery organizing tool it is, enabling chaos to course through its predetermined order. She perceives Kelly's randomized color as slyly introducing seeds of disruption into the ordering device. She and Higgins both aided us in understanding the collages as works finding their internal coherence through their contradictions—the countervailing forces of a rigid geometric order and the anarchy of color. Despite the rules-driven nature of this series, neither Kelly's process nor the grid can make color come to heel.

To view *Spectrum Colors Arranged by Chance* in this light is to see a series engaged not only with chance but also with aesthetic risk. Part of Kelly's gambit in this series was to open his work to "gauche" color combinations that continue to lend the works an inherent strangeness and an alluring mischievous air. Giampaolo and I, as hosts and conveners, attempted to organize a conversation that would allow these crucial aspects of the works to come into focus—to see the works, in a sense, as they were before we knew them so well. To do so requires a loosening of certain ideological commitments, which offers its own benefits. It may be that in our own time we are newly able to see these works in relation to their inherently vital and precarious moment of transatlantic experimentation. Along with this, we can see the social, the human, and the transcendental as realms that are not excluded from Kelly's grids but rather are concomitant with them. These private, humble, and colossally ambitious works have slowly become more visible to the public over the past seventy years, allowing us to regard them with a fuller sense of the strengths and vulnerabilities they possess—qualities that, already in 1954, Ellsworth Kelly understood would be important to save.

1   Prior to this exhibition, the collages *Spectrum Colors Arranged by Chance II*, *Spectrum Colors Arranged by Chance VI*, and *Spectrum Colors Arranged by Chance VII* were displayed together in 1992–93 as part of *Ellsworth Kelly: The Years in France, 1948–1954* at the Galerie Nationale du Jeu de Paume, Paris; the Westfälisches Landesmuseum, Münster; and the National Gallery of Art, Washington, DC. Additionally, in 1999, the Art Institute of Chicago presented the collages *Spectrum Colors Arranged by Chance IV, Spectrum Colors Arranged by Chance VI*, and *Spectrum Colors Arranged by Chance VII* in the exhibition *Ellsworth Kelly: The Early Drawings, 1948–1955* (see fig. 1).

2   For an introduction to Bois's writings on Kelly's early works, see "Ellsworth Kelly in France: Anti-Composition in Its Many Guises," in Yve-Alain Bois, Jack Cowart, and Alfred Pacquement, *Ellsworth Kelly: The Years in France, 1948–1954*, exh. cat. (Washington, DC: National Gallery of Art, 1992), 9–36; and Yve-Alain Bois, *Ellsworth Kelly: Catalogue Raisonné of Paintings, Reliefs, and Sculpture* vol. 1, *1940–1953*, ed. Eric Banks (Paris: Cahiers d'Art, 2015).

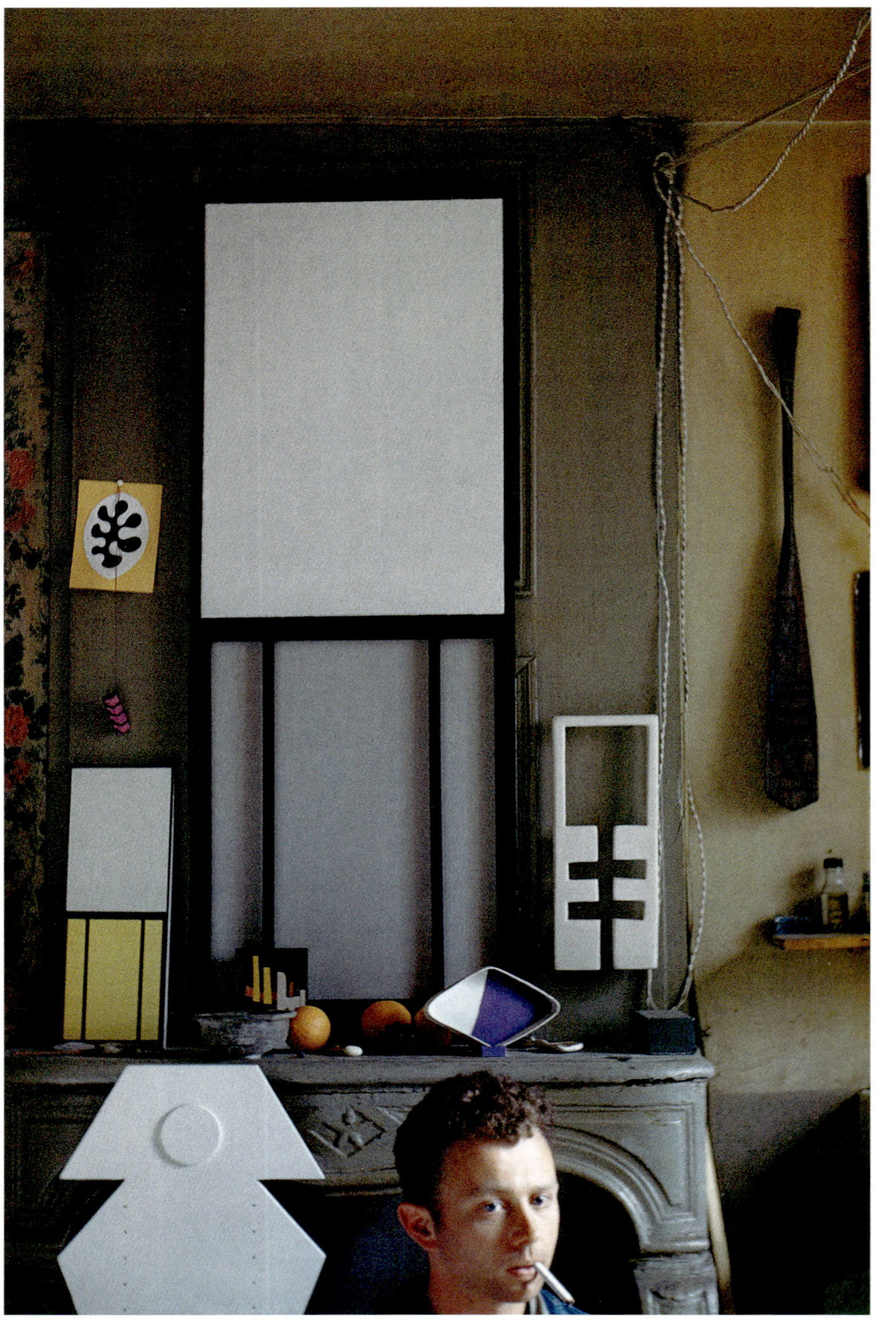

Fig. 7.   Ellsworth Kelly in his studio at the Hôtel de Bourgogne, Paris, April 1950, with works including *Window, Museum of Modern Art, Paris* (1949) on the mantle behind him.

Step Back and Let It Happen: A Roundtable on Ellsworth Kelly's *Spectrum Colors Arranged by Chance*

With Giampaolo Bianconi, Caitlin Haskell, Hannah B Higgins, Jacqueline Humphries, and Jack Shear

Roundtable

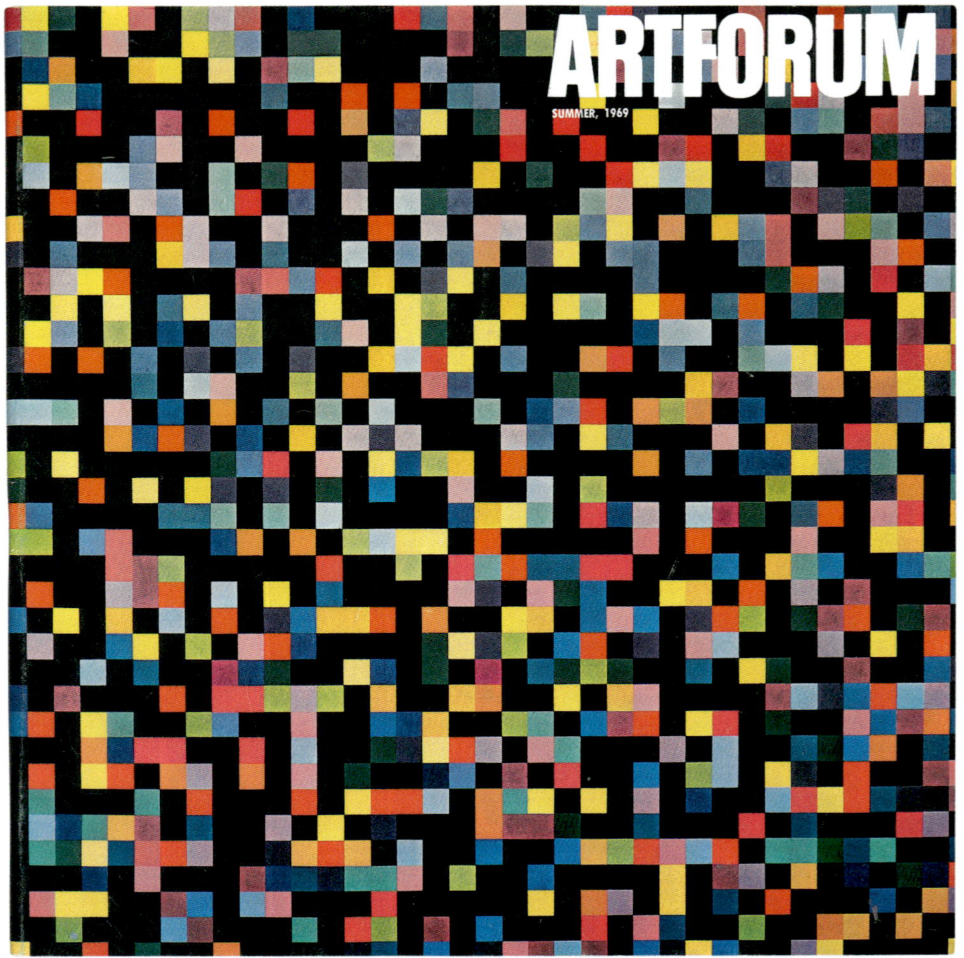

Fig. 8. Cover of *Artforum* 7, no. 10 (Summer 1969), featuring
Ellsworth Kelly's *Spectrum Colors Arranged by Chance* (1953; pp. 66–67).

This conversation took place on July 10, 2024, in the
galleries of the Art Institute of Chicago on the occasion
of the exhibition *Ellsworth Kelly: Spectrum Colors
Arranged by Chance* (June 22–September 9, 2024).
The text has been edited by Giampaolo Bianconi for
length and clarity.

JACK SHEAR
Ellsworth lived in Paris from 1948 to 1954. He got sick in 1954, so he telegraphed his parents and said, "I need $200 for my passage back to New York, and I need another $200 to bring back all the works that I've made." His parents sent him $200 and told him to leave the works there.

Ellsworth asked around at all the shipping companies in Paris until he learned that the Cunard Line would allow him to ship the works on credit. Cunard held on to the works until Ellsworth repaid the $200 shipping cost, which he paid in five-dollar weekly installments. When he made his last payment, the Cunard employee said, "We're going to miss you, Mr. Kelly."

The works he made in Paris (see fig. 7), including the *Spectrum Colors* collages, were very precious to Ellsworth, and he knew how important they were.

CAITLIN HASKELL
Yet, interestingly, the works would not find a broad audience until many years later. What I found striking in looking back at the works' reception is that the *Spectrum Colors* series did not really become known publicly until the late 1960s. John Coplans wrote about the works in the summer 1969 issue of *Artforum*, and the painting, *Spectrum Colors Arranged by Chance* (pp. 66–67), was featured on the cover (fig. 8).[1] There is a sense that the collages were a treasure trove, a private store of ideas for Ellsworth. It is almost as if they were a special source that he could draw from, that supplied ideas for many years of work moving forward, but one that remained out of circulation for most of the 1950s and 1960s.

JACQUELINE HUMPHRIES
I see Ellsworth as a bridge figure connecting his time with more radical ideas about art making while shying away from the more ideological, dogmatic side of that. He slyly reasserted in art a kind of lyrical sensibility, which came in under the umbrella of the de-skilled, the generic, the automatic, or chance.

HANNAH B HIGGINS
In the literature, Ellsworth's connection with Jean Arp comes up frequently. But several scholars have suggested that the artist whom Ellsworth was really interested in was Sophie Taeuber-Arp (see fig. 9).[2] For me, the way that she explored space and Ellsworth tightened it brings up a compelling set of questions.

HASKELL
Taeuber-Arp is an interesting kindred spirit in some ways. But with Ellsworth there are also so many false cognates, whether it is Ben Nicholson or Georges Vantongerloo—comparisons where something seems similar visually but has an entirely different motivation.

What I find particularly special about the *Spectrum Colors* series, which you can pick up on through the writings of scholars such as Yve-Alain Bois, is a sense of the motivation. There are so many possible readings of the collages, and they can go in lots of different directions if you let go of a sense of what is driving them.

HIGGINS
I, like so many others, have thought of these works in relation to Piet Mondrian. But it was striking for me to see that by the early 1970s, most critics were saying that the Mondrian association was a mistake.[3] In a sense, that tells us about Mondrian's reception by American critics. Late Mondrian was bad, and these works look

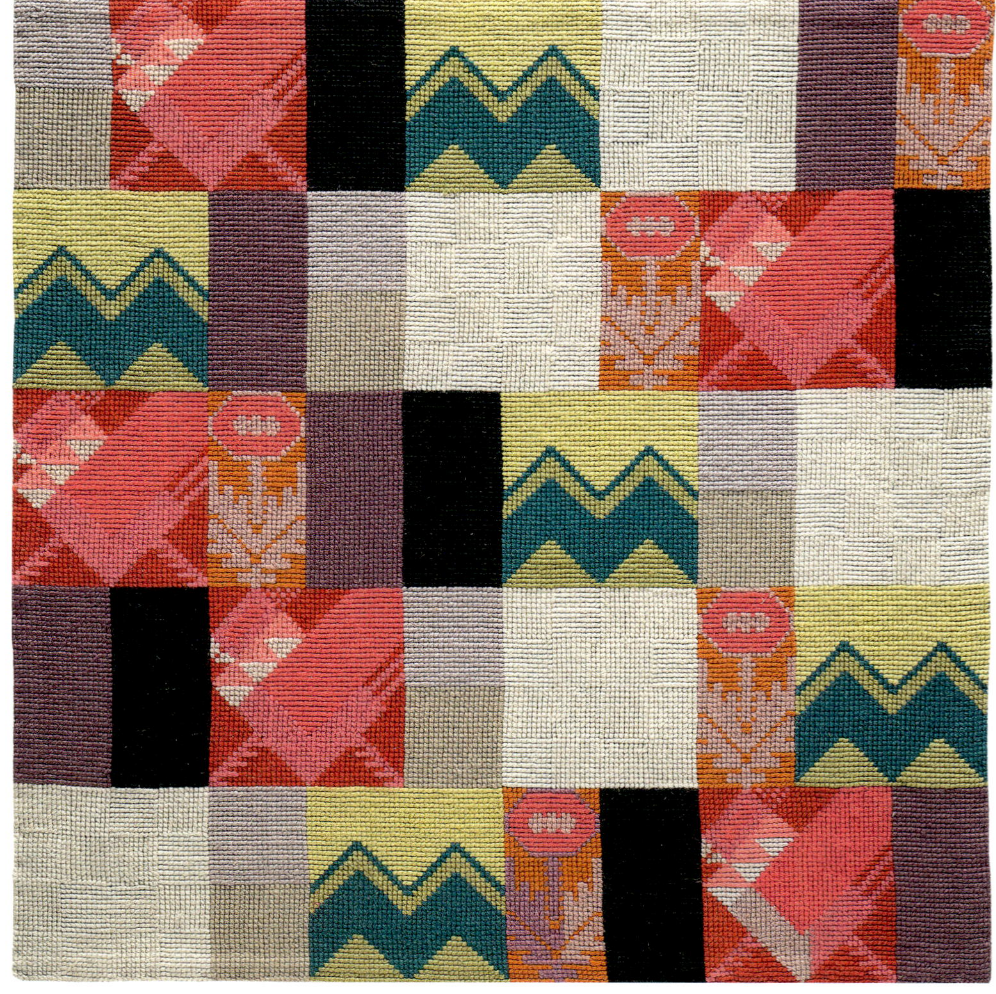

Fig. 9. Sophie Taeuber-Arp (Swiss, 1889–1943). *Cushion Panel*, 1916.
Wool on canvas; 53 × 52 cm (20⅞ × 20½ in.). Museum für Gestaltung, Zürcher
Hochschule der Künste, Zurich.

more like late Mondrian—his *Broadway Boogie Woogie* (1942–43; The Museum of Modern Art, New York), for example, which is all about adjacency of color.

HASKELL
What do you imagine it would have been like to look at these works in the time of their making?

HIGGINS
Mondrian was low-hanging fruit. His grids limit the impact of color one to the next, so they are the opposite of Ellsworth's. Ellsworth clearly was anxious about returning to New York and being compared endlessly to Mondrian.

HASKELL
So, in 1951, there seem to have been only missteps for the viewer looking at these collages?

HIGGINS
The German philosopher Hans-Georg Gadamer wrote about the concept of the horizon, basically saying, "Here is what people can know at a specific moment in time based on their context—that is, the world around them. People are conditioned to see things a certain way. But of course, contexts shift, so we find new meanings in things over time."[4] It is a forgiving way of thinking about what, in retrospect, might seem like absurd missteps.

HASKELL
Exactly. With the benefit of history, we can look at a much broader range of references and related practices, or interests in related questions. We know, for example, that Robert Rauschenberg was making his *White Paintings* at the same time that Ellsworth was making *Spectrum Colors*. And René Magritte, in an entirely different way, was also thinking about

making an anonymous type of painting, removing one's subjective self from a picture.

When I step back and try to put myself into this midcentury moment, and what could be known during that period, I tend to go to a much earlier set of reference points. I think about Paul Cezanne's constructive stroke, which is relatively the same size and scale as one of the colored squares in the *Spectrum Colors* collages. But there is a tipping point where Cezanne's stroke, despite its insistently abstract and material qualities, clearly becomes part of an image. Conversely, with Ellsworth's work, you are left questioning whether there is something pictorial to be seen. Are there images or portions of images to be perceived, or is it entirely abstract?

SHEAR
It is telling that, in 1954, when Ellsworth saw a review in *ARTnews* of Ad Reinhardt's paintings at the Betty Parsons Gallery,[5] he thought, "Maybe now I can return to the United States, because if work such as this is being shown there, then there might be receptivity to my work." Betty Parsons would become Ellsworth's dealer in New York in 1956.

GIAMPAOLO BIANCONI
To me, Ellsworth, at least a side of him, was a kind of American Neo-Concrete artist. There is also something in the form of his works that is transatlantic. I imagine one of the reasons Bois was such a perfect audience for Ellsworth's work was because Bois's circle included several South American artists who lived in Paris, including Lygia Clark and Sérgio de Camargo. Somehow Ellsworth's work makes more sense in light of its history with Concrete art.

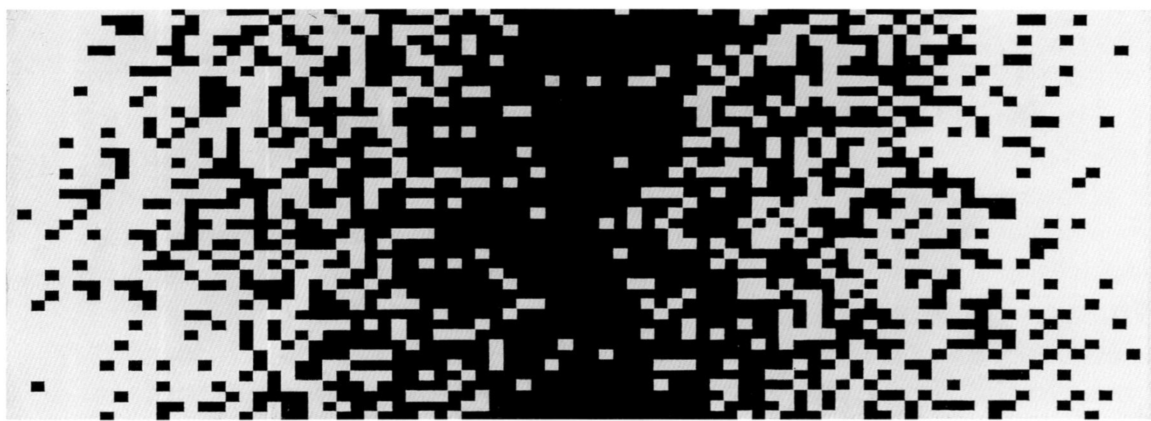

Fig. 10.   Ellsworth Kelly (American, 1923–2015). *Seine*, 1951. Oil on wood; 41.9 × 114.9 cm (16½ × 45¼ in.). Philadelphia Museum of Art, purchased with funds contributed in memory of Anne d'Harnoncourt and other Museum Funds, 2008-228-1.

SHEAR
Ellsworth described himself
as an American artist. He
would say, "I am an American,
therefore I am an American
artist." The French thought
Ellsworth was too American,
and the Americans thought
Ellsworth was too French.

HUMPHRIES
In looking at the nine *Spectrum
Colors* collages, I am struck
by the notion that a grid is
never just a grid. Each of these
collages has a pictorial feeling.
Within the structure of the grid,
you have all these possibilities,
from the black and white
rectangles of *Seine* (1951; fig. 10),
to more compositional grids, to
random-seeming arrangements,
as in *Spectrum Colors Arranged
by Chance VI* (pp. 58–59), before
moving into more decoration
or design, as you see in the last
three collages. The grid even
brings us to the present with
digital images and pixelation.
It is a universal scaffolding.

HIGGINS
Grids produce absolute order and
the ability to see disorder, and
we can use the information that
the grid gives us in the abstract.

SHEAR
Think of the art being made in
the US at the time—a Jackson
Pollock all-over painting, for
example. How does a grid such
as Ellsworth's *Colors for a Large
Wall* get put next to a Pollock?
The Museum of Modern Art
initially put that painting, which
Ellsworth made in 1951, in the
room featuring artworks from
the 1960s. They didn't know
where to put it. Kirk Varnedoe
was the first curator who took it
out of that room and put it next
to a Barnett Newman (see fig. 11).

HUMPHRIES
All the ideas in painting were

coming from Europe at the
time. Ellsworth was in Paris,
but he was not looking at art.
He was looking at the city's
drain grates, chimneys, and
industrial design. For me, the
Spectrum Colors collages are
about him coming to a new
understanding of color, a
subjectivity of color with which
he put aside decisions about
composition and artistic vision
for pure discovery. But he did
not continue making works like
them. Even with *Colors for a
Large Wall*, there is an essential
shift from the collages, with his
use of the individual canvases.

SHEAR
He solved a problem and moved
on. He did that with a number
of works.

HIGGINS
I agree the problem was solved,
but the color adjacencies in
the *Spectrum Colors* collages
nevertheless evoke a surprise,
maybe of the kind we now
associate with readymades or
with John Cage's interest in
indeterminacy. Bois has written
about the anti-compositional
thread in Ellsworth's work as
moving from the grid toward
bilateral symmetry and other
aspects of an "interstitial
surface" that, while not a grid of
colored squares, nevertheless
undermine the undecidability
of the figure/ground opposition
effectively explored in *Colors for
a Large Wall*.[6]

SHEAR
I like the bracketing of these
particular works between *Seine*,
which was done by chance, and
Colors for a Large Wall. They fit
between those.

HASKELL
Would it be worth considering
some of the similarities and
differences between the first

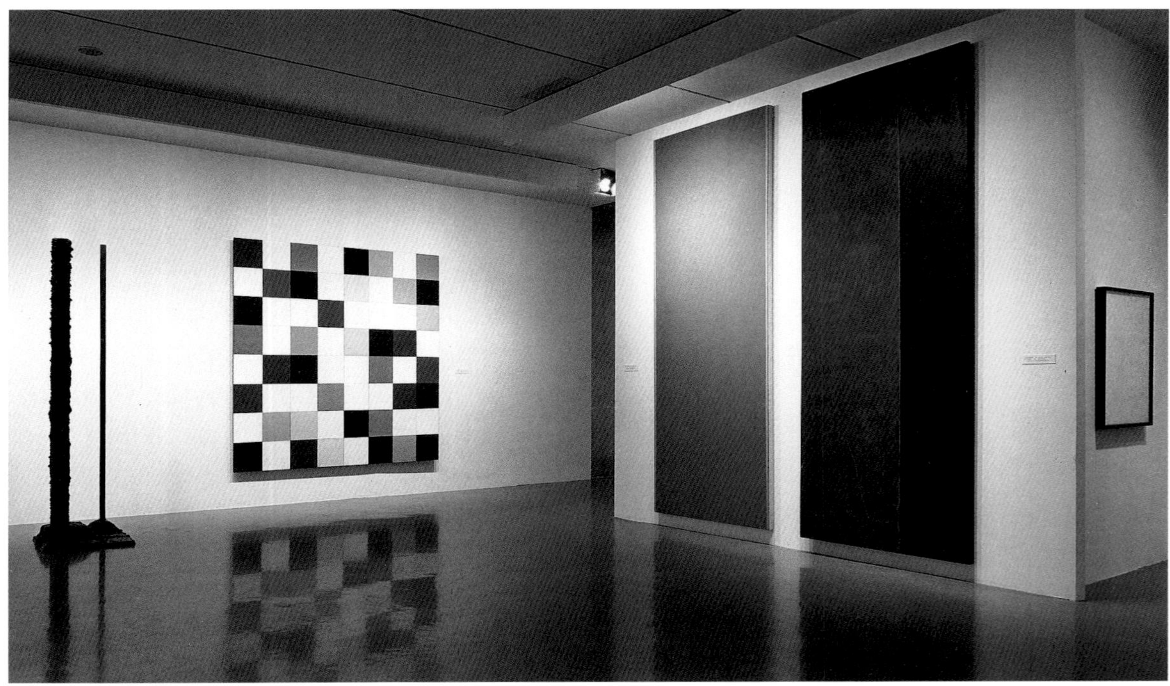

Fig. 11. Installation view of the exhibition *Art of the Real*, the Museum of Modern Art, New York, July 3–September 8, 1968, with (left to right) Barnett Newman's *Here* (1950), Ellsworth Kelly's *Colors for a Large Wall* (1951), Barnett Newman's *Day One* (1951) and *Ulysses* (1952), and Jasper Johns's *White Numbers* (1957).

Spectrum Colors collage and *Seine*? They both have an elongated rectangular format. Maybe that format takes us from the black-and-white painted binary system of *Seine* to the collaged grids we have here in the gallery with us.

BIANCONI
Seine is systematically similar to the *Spectrum Colors* collages, but that comes from an act of looking, as is the case with much of Ellsworth's work. Suggesting that the latter is representational would be going too far, but between *Seine* and the collages, there is an idea of translating something into something else.

Yet the collages move away from that sense of seeing. In the desire for their anonymity, one of the detours that this series takes us through is a movement away from Ellsworth's own eye, which defines so much of his abstraction.

SHEAR
He was trying to be impersonal. The commercial papers he used in the collages are readymades, or "already-mades."

BIANCONI
Ellsworth's collages are more about the object and less about the color chart. This is what distinguishes them from other lineages of ready-made color and painting such as Marcel Duchamp's *Tu m'* (1918; fig. 12), where there is a color chart, or Rauschenberg's *Rebus* (1955; fig. 13), which is very much about industrial progression.

HUMPHRIES
Ellsworth saw one of Duchamp's *Rotoreliefs* for the first time in 1950 or so.[7] Interestingly, the *Rotoreliefs*, made early in the twentieth century, were not taken forward historically by other artists until midcentury.

After the two world wars, American and European artists were picking up the threads, with new ideas about what must change and what must be reflected in art making.

HASKELL
In the context of the 1950s, there is a strong sense of artists wanting to get rid of old habits— enough with the tendencies and behaviors of art that had been passed down through the Western tradition for so long. But Ellsworth did not get rid of everything. There is still something retained.

SHEAR
Ellsworth went to art school at the Museum of Fine Arts in Boston. He drew and painted from the nude, and he loved the museum's twelfth-century Catalonian chapel frescoes. There were Monets hanging in the assistants' rooms, and he would ask, "Why aren't those in the galleries?"

When Minimalism was on the rise, artists were very literate in terms of describing what they were doing and what they wanted to do. But Ellsworth was not going to tell you what a work is or is not about; he wanted you to use your eyes and look at it. He famously said, "If you can turn off the mind and look only with the eyes, ultimately everything becomes abstract."[8]

HIGGINS
Is there something posthuman about these works? When I came into the gallery, I experienced a feeling of familiarity.

BIANCONI
I am not sure there is anything posthuman in them, but I defin- itely sense a desire of the artist to escape from himself in the process of making them.

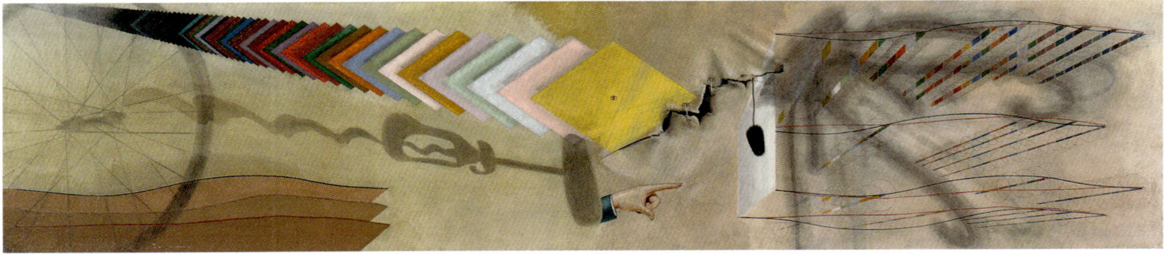

Fig. 12.   Marcel Duchamp (American, born France, 1887–1968). *Tu m'*, 1918. Oil on canvas, with bottlebrush, safety pins, and bolt; 69.8 × 303 cm (27½ × 119⁵⁄₁₆ in.). Yale University Art Gallery, gift of the Estate of Katherine S. Dreier, 1953.6.4.

SHEAR
Every time a craftsperson
makes something, it isn't
always impersonal. Ellsworth
talked about watching stone-
masons work, placing pieces
of stones in relationship to
one another. It may seem like
an anonymous process, but
really it's not. There is intention
in that work; the stonemason
decided which stones to
place where.

HASKELL
If we go back to Ellsworth's
processes and to Jack's point
about problem solving, we can
see specific areas in these works
where decisions were made.
The grid of *Seine* consists of
black and white rectangles, forty
high and eighty wide. In the first
collage of this series, *Spectrum
Colors Arranged by Chance I* (pp.
48–49), each of the two joined
papers has a twenty-by-twenty
grid of squares, resulting in a
twenty-by-forty rectangular grid
overall. But *Seine* and *Spectrum
Colors Arranged by Chance I*
show a similar approach, with
the density of rectangles or
squares being sparsest on either
side and increasing toward
the center.

Then, if we look at
*Spectrum Colors Arranged by
Chance II* (pp. 50–51; see also
fig. 15), another decision is
apparent. There are four joined
pieces of paper, not two, each
with a grid of nineteen by
nineteen, making it thirty-
eight by thirty-eight overall. In
*Spectrum Colors Arranged by
Chance III* (pp. 52–53), the overall
grid remains thirty-eight by
thirty-eight, but it is on a single
sheet of paper. The grid units
remain the same size as we
move from the third collage to
the fourth, but in the latter (pp.
54–55), the introduction of black
eliminates a traditional sense
of figure and ground.

SHEAR
In that work, *Spectrum Colors
Arranged by Chance IV*, there is
a margin of black that does
not appear in the subsequent
collages.

HASKELL
*Spectrum Colors Arranged by
Chance V* (pp. 56–57) has a more
balanced distribution of color
throughout; the issue of everything being too concentrated at
center is resolved. As Giampaolo
has pointed out, *Spectrum
Colors Arranged by Chance VI*
(pp. 58–59) is perhaps the most
balanced within the series. It
again has a grid of thirty-eight
by thirty-eight, meaning there
are 1,444 squares. Ellsworth
divided that number by two
and selected 722 black units.
Each of the eighteen colors
of the *papier gommette* is
represented by approximately
forty squares, and Ellsworth,
through his chance-based
process, determined where, for
example, all the yellow squares
would go, then where all the
dark blue squares would go,
and so on. It is a truly mathe-
matically balanced piece, even
though the placement of the
colors was random.

In *Spectrum Colors
Arranged by Chance VII* (pp.
60–61), there is no longer a black
or white ground, if you will, and
the grid increases, returning
to forty by forty. The last two
collages, the eighth and ninth
(pp. 62–63, 64–65), are separate;
they stand apart from the others
because the size of the unit in
the grid has grown significantly,
as we can see. This is all to say
that there are several problems
being solved, though not
ultimately resolved, throughout
the series. Choices were made
in the making of these non-
compositional works, and we
can point to deliberate decisions
that informed an aesthetic result.

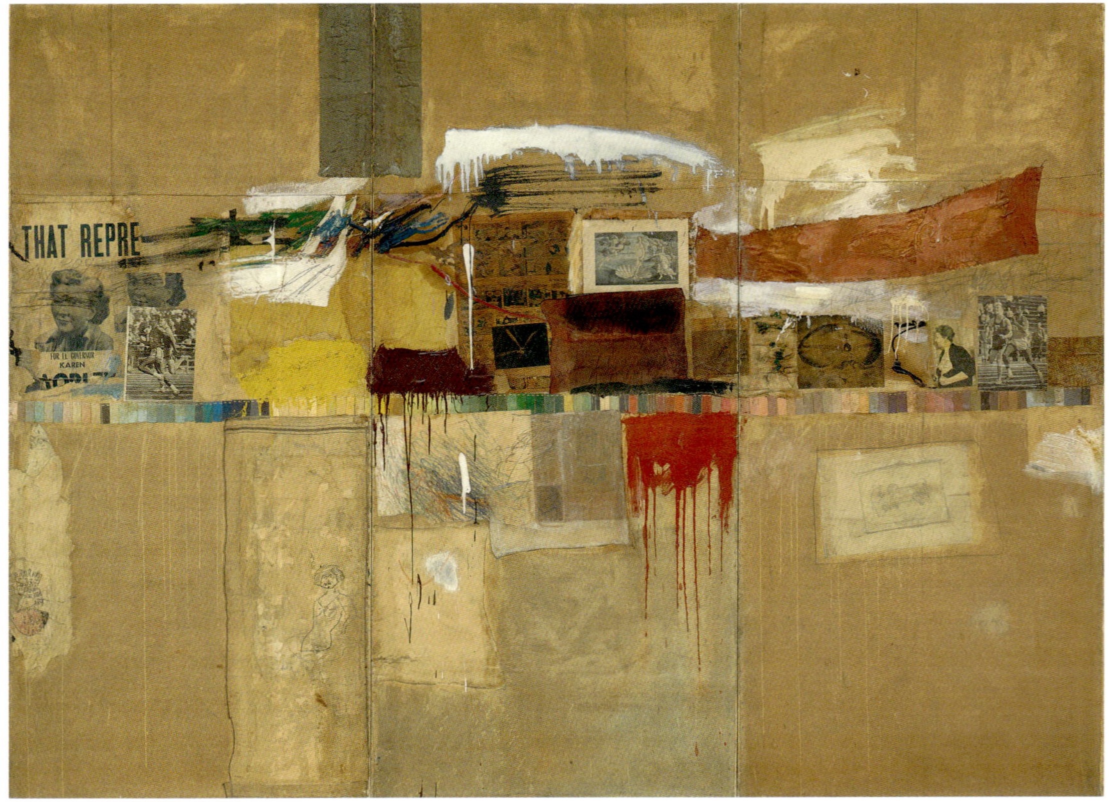

Fig. 13.   Robert Rauschenberg (American, 1925–2008). *Rebus*, 1955. Oil, alkyd paint, pencil, crayon, pastel, cut-and-pasted printed and painted papers, and fabric on canvas mounted and stapled to fabric; 3 panels; 243.8 × 333.1 cm (96 × 131⅛ in.). The Museum of Modern Art, New York, partial and promised gift of Jo Carole and Ronald S. Lauder and bequest of Virginia C. Field, gift of Mr. and Mrs. Peter A. Rübel, and gift of Jay R. Braus (all by exchange), 243.2005.a–c.

HUMPHRIES
It summons the classical
dichotomy between linear
perspective and the material
accumulation of masses of
paint. American art flipped the
standard priority; mass became
more important than line.
Ellsworth cut out shapes, and
the discarded scraps are what
he made into art—using the very
weight of color and form as a
material. That was a very sly
way of bringing mass in as *the*
defining mechanism rather than
a defining mechanism.

SHEAR
Most contemporary artists are
mark makers. Ellsworth was
classically trained to draw and
paint from the nude and to
study what was in front of him.
I think draftsmanship is what
Ellsworth and Henri Matisse had
in common. Ellsworth was a great
admirer of Matisse's work, esp-
ecially the late cutouts, but he did
not like being compared to him.

HASKELL
That is interesting because
Matisse's cutouts are basically
contemporaneous with the
Spectrum Colors collages.
When I look at the collages
today, I occasionally think there
is a sense of finesse in the colors,
yet the colors are ready-made.
Sometimes I find a particularly
nice cut on one of the *papiers
gommettes,* but of course, we
are not supposed to appreciate
that. It is meant to be an
anonymous gesture.

HIGGINS
I am also interested in the
quality of the cut. I imagine
Ellsworth with his scissors,
making straight cuts, versus
the curves of Matisse's cuts,
and what it would be like to
spend the day making those
cuts and assembling the cut
papers. Envisioning the process
brings me back to your point,
Jacqueline, about pixelation.

During his service in World
War II, Ellsworth designed
camouflage (see fig. 14).[9] That is
incredibly interesting because
camouflage is in a way fully
abstract but also cannot be
a thing. It is about deception.

HUMPHRIES
Even the decisions made before
the execution of these works
brought their own subjectivity
with them. Why use more black
in this one, less white in that
one? The ready-made paper also
contains subjectivity.

I want to bring up the
larger ideas of self-erasure
and self-annihilation, and the
thin line between the two. The
highly experimental nature of
the *Spectrum Colors* works
introduces a kind of moral and
ethical valence that is full of
questions. Having been made
not long after the horrible wars,
these works raise questions
about subjectivity and what it
means to be human, to be
male, to be female, to be gay,
to be straight.

Now we have machines that
are capable of doing many things
that humans can do. These
machines have taken away
creative outlets. From Dada
and Surrealism to the artificial
intelligence of the present, there
seems to be a desire for self-
erasure, or is it self-annihilation?

BIANCONI
The history of twentieth-century
art is an entanglement between
subjectivity and self-erasure—
wanting things to come from a
place that cannot be controlled
yet having that be managed.
Artists tried to do something
automatic, but the work retains
their mark. They attempted to
move beyond themselves with
all the decisions they delegated
and the strategies of chance

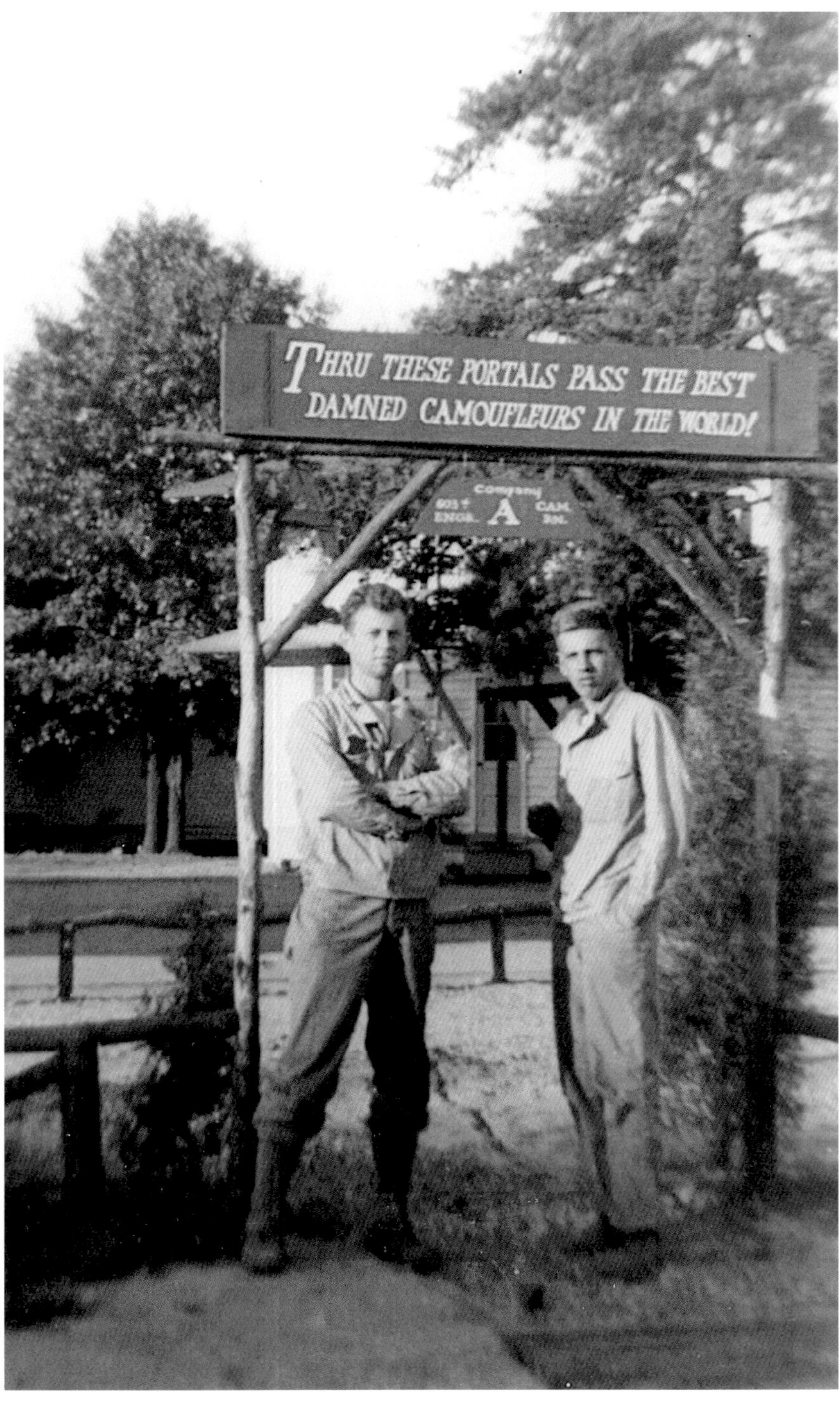

Fig. 14.   Ellsworth Kelly and Elmer Mellebrand, Camp des Loges, Saint-Germain-en-Laye, France, 1943, under a sign that reads, "Thru these portals pass the best damned camoufleurs in the world!"

they used. But they still ended up making something iterable and identifiable. There is a quality of that in these works.

HIGGINS
Artists gave the obligation to the viewer. They could go only so far because the viewer will render the work in their mind and for themselves.

HUMPHRIES
The more one tries to banish the human or what is thought of as irredeemably corrupt about being human, the more human one becomes, in a sense.

HASKELL
And there is still an autographic mark: Pollock's drip is tied to Pollock; Willem de Kooning's stroke is tied to de Kooning. One of the big shifts that took place—for example, between the previous gallery of Abstract Expressionist works of the 1940s and 1950s and this gallery— was the desire to move toward anonymity in a way that is less autographic than Surrealist automatic processes. That is one reason why the use of a system was so important to the *Spectrum Colors* series.

HIGGINS
In his 1957 essay "Chance-Imagery," George Brecht depersonalizes Pollock completely, describing the artist's action painting as chance based, which to us today seems almost absurd.[10] Chance imagery described unintended, or not directly controlled, dimensions of Pollock's expressionism. Chance imagery has the rejection of direct control in common with Kelly, even if aspects of its allover design might appear to have something in common with the American Expressionists. The ready-made aleatoric aspect of the work,

on the other hand, suggests something very different. Brecht later found this in Cage.

BIANCONI
Ellsworth's anonymity is perhaps not one of obliteration but perhaps that of a kind of craftsperson. There is a public dimension to a lot of his abstraction. The self-fashioning in these collages ends up going in a somewhat architectural direction, which is paradoxical given the fragility of the works, as they are literally held together by Ellsworth's saliva. Yet this body of work led to the architectural *Colors for a Large Wall,* and the lineage of these works ends up in Ellsworth's building and larger-scale projects (see fig. 17).

HIGGINS
Was the arrangement of the canvases of *Colors for a Large Wall* variable?

SHEAR
No. At one point, Ellsworth declared the configuration to be set. However, viewers are welcome to rearrange the colored squares in their minds.

HUMPHRIES
If he had left the configuration open, the risk would be that someone could arrange the squares to form more of a picture. Even though the configuration of the colors is random, their arrangement has to be set in stone to retain the work's openness.

BIANCONI
To me, one of the most noticeable things about the *Spectrum Colors* works is how strange many of the color combinations are. They might feel familiar to us today, but when these works were made, I wonder if some of the resulting

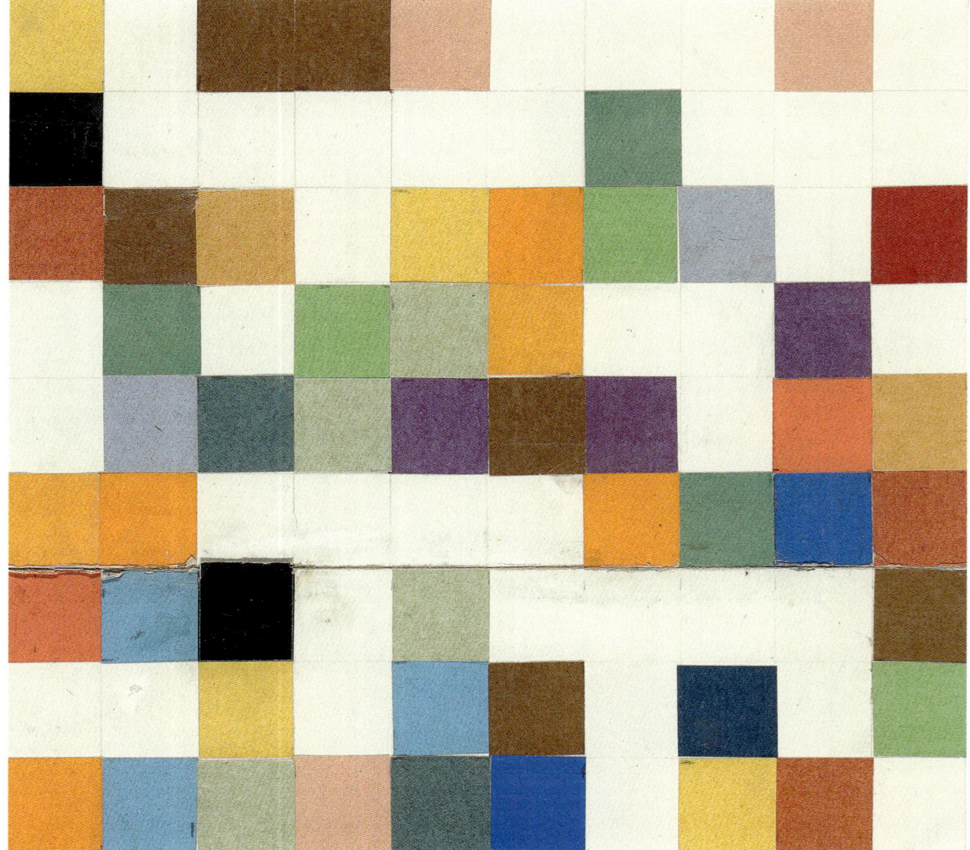

Fig. 15.   Ellsworth Kelly. *Spectrum Colors Arranged by Chance II* (detail),
1951. Collage on paper; 97.2 × 97.2 cm (38¼ × 38¼ in.). The Museum
of Modern Art, New York, purchased with funds provided by Jo Carole
and Ronald S. Lauder, 500.1997.

color adjacencies were jarring—
orange and pink, for example.

SHEAR
Orange and pink recall the
fourteenth-century painting
of the Virgin and Child by
Ambrogio Lorenzetti in the
Museum of Fine Arts, Boston,
in which the Virgin wears
orange and the baby Jesus
wears pink.[11] Ellsworth made
a copy of this painting, but his
mother destroyed it.

HIGGINS
As part of his art school training,
Ellsworth had to study Albert
Munsell's color theory, yet
the *Spectrum Colors* works
are clearly a repudiation of
that. I find myself wondering
if, in France, Ellsworth had an
epiphany about the philosophy
of color, leading to a different
approach to it, one that is
neither mechanistic nor chromo-
luminescent.

SHEAR
Ellsworth used to tell a story
about running into Josef Albers,
who had just seen Ellsworth's
exhibition at the Sidney Janis
Gallery on East Fifty-Seventh
Street in Manhattan in 1967.
*Spectrum Colors Arranged by
Chance II* was in the show, and
Albers asked Ellsworth which
color theory he used for it.
Ellsworth told him that he did
not use one, that his approach
was intuitive. Albers replied,
"Well, it looks like it," and
walked away.

That is what Ellsworth was
fighting against. He did not need
a theory to do what he wanted
to do; he did not want to explain
why particular colors "go"
together. He did not want to
write down formulas on the back
of each work, unlike many of the
artists working in abstraction,
who felt the need to codify what
they were doing.

HUMPHRIES
It is interesting that, with the
painting, he memorialized
*Spectrum Colors Arranged
by Chance VI*. But if I were not
familiar with the painting and
saw it in a museum or a gallery,
I am not sure that I would
immediately recognize it as
an Ellsworth Kelly. Yet it is a
springboard for so much in
his work.

BIANCONI
My theory about why Ellsworth
chose *Spectrum Colors Arranged
by Chance VI* for the painting
is that, as Caitlin mentioned
earlier, it is the most balanced
of the collages in terms of
composition. In each collage,
he was testing different modes
of distributing the squares; the
distribution in *Spectrum Colors
Arranged by Chance VI* is the
most even and allover. From
there, the subsequent collages
go in a different direction.

HASKELL
The black squares in *Spectrum
Colors Arranged by Chance VI*
do tend to form into shapes
that could be read as signs—
quasi-icons or pixelated
symbols, if you will. By the
ninth collage, that possibility
has been eliminated.

HIGGINS
In *Spectrum Colors Arranged
by Chance VII*, it is almost as if
Ellsworth realized that when
he removed the black, it was
maybe too much, too decadent.

Jacqueline, when you
were beginning to contemplate
your own theories or thoughts
about color and referentiality
of color, did you think about
Ellsworth Kelly?

HUMPHRIES
Color is a problem because of
taste and subjectivity—pretty
colors, ugly colors. It pulls you in

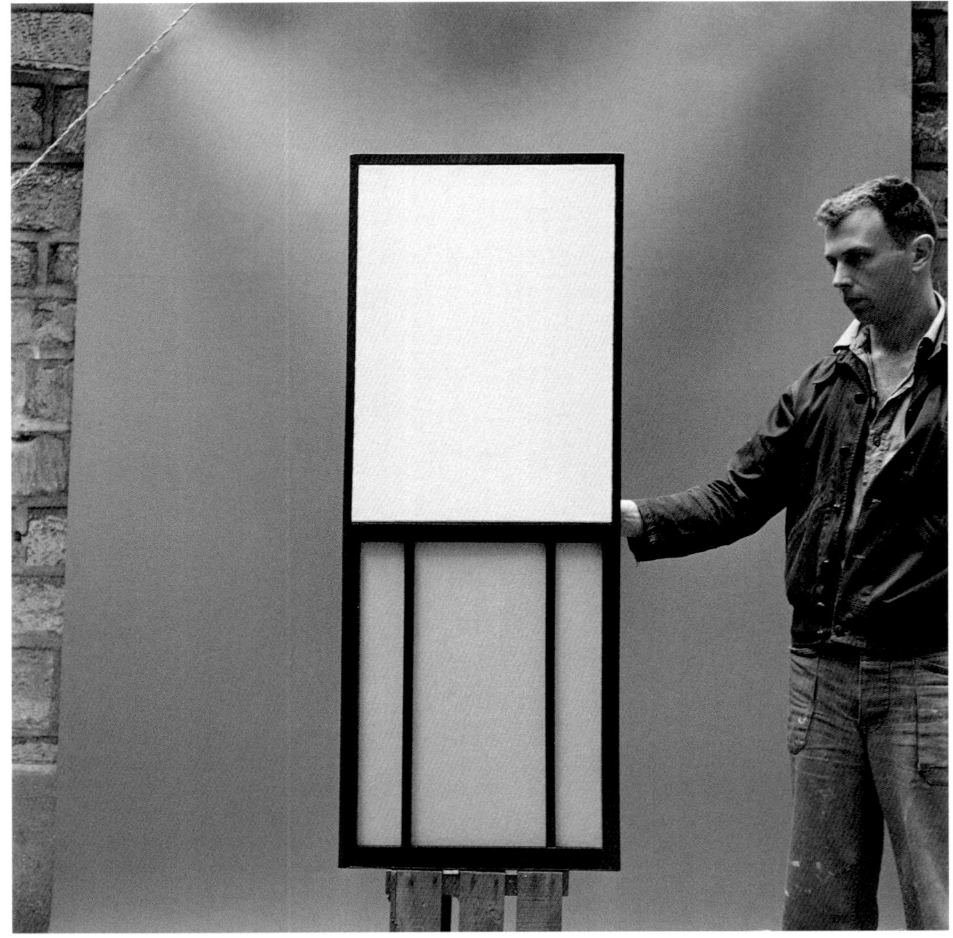

Fig. 16.   Ellsworth Kelly with *Window, Museum of Modern Art, Paris* (1949), Paris, 1950.

all these different directions. For Matisse and the Fauves, color was wild, stochastic energy. Interestingly, the *Spectrum Colors* collages followed a number of mostly black-and-white works for Ellsworth—for example, *Window, Museum of Modern Art, Paris* (1949; see fig. 16) and *Toilette* (1949; private collection), the Turkish toilet. After those it seems as though he decided to confront the problem of color.

I would describe myself as a chromophobe, and because color is something I struggle with, I look for ways to mobilize it. The process of choosing colors is challenging, which is why artists need guides— nature or the figure or the color spectrum itself, for example. Color selection is not just about choosing colors one likes or doesn't like.

HASKELL
I like how you described mobilizing color—letting color lead the way.

HUMPHRIES
A color coming out of a paint tube is not necessarily the final color; it is a pigment that can be mixed with other pigments to create a different color. With *papier gommette*, the color has been made for you, and you encounter it in its own spirit. Each paper is a ready-made color.

SHEAR
Ellsworth said that he always mixed his paints; he never used them straight out of the tube. He would even add red or blue or yellow to his whites and blacks.

In these collages, because the colored papers are fugitive, the colors we see now are likely duller than they were when the works were made.

BIANCONI
Seeing these works gives us a strong sense of their physicality. There are traces of Ellsworth's DNA on them; he licked the individual papers to get them to stick. In the literature, his physical engagement with these works sometimes gets a bit lost in the intellectual project. But his physical engagement ultimately led to works that in turn make the viewer physically engage with color.

HUMPHRIES
It is interesting to think about using formal systems as a kind of relative liberation: finding freedom through the confines. Because, with a system, you do not have to think; certain decisions are made for you. Your conscious mindset is set on the task of following directions while your unconscious and the objective conditions are allowing another thing to happen that you could not have made occur through willful decisions.

HIGGINS
This brings me back to posthumanism, which I had mentioned earlier. Post-humanism is not against the contributions of human beings; rather, posthumanism says reason cannot exist in isolation, whereas reason is the defining feature of the human being in a Cartesian, rational place. Posthumanism resists philosophical Cartesianism.

HUMPHRIES
What could be more rational than the grid, yet here it is being instrumentalized as a force of its own opposite.

HASKELL
Perhaps we should step outside of Cartesian reason when we look at these works.

Kasimir Malevich, for example, understood geometric painting as aligned with something cosmic and spiritual, something more powerful and bigger than oneself. We have talked about the works here in terms of post-humanism and self-erasure as well as in terms of having a crafted, bodily aspect to them. These seem at odds, but perhaps they do not have to be.

HIGGINS
I am thinking of a tradition such as American transcendentalism, which resonates strongly with the Buddhist sense of there being living, spiritual content in nature. You cannot make a clear divide between, say, a human being and the natural world. I would prefer not to see posthumanism and self-erasure in opposition but to see their history as being treated in opposition. People feel that they need to choose a side. In a 2003 essay, Howard Singerman briefly mentions Conceptual art.[12] If my memory serves, he says that this body of work is on both sides of these historical tendencies. That, to me, is a useful way to think about them, as being together, not necessarily in opposition.

BIANCONI
When these works were made, a computer was a big, clunky machine that you used your whole body to operate with punch cards. As a tool, it is not so different from Kelly's tool: a system whose use involves not only the mind but the whole body. It has a physical presence.

SHEAR
At Ellsworth's memorial, I called him a "transcendental anarchist." He loved transc-endentalism, and he was an anarchist.

HIGGINS
He would have shared that with Cage. In describing their friendship, people tend to think of chance operations or Zen. But Cage too was interested in the transcendentalists and certainly the anarchists.

SHEAR
Their connection was more Taoist in that chance is what happens to us every day, and we either accept it or not.

HUMPHRIES
In order to see things truly, one has to get out of the way.

SHEAR
Step back and let it happen.

HIGGINS
What if in this body of work there is a message to us at this time, one relating to hyper-individualism and the inability to think socially? As Jacqueline and Jack were saying, we need to step back, not necessarily blow up the world in front of us.

HASKELL
This again is making me think about the different ways that these works have been described and what people saw in them at different junctures. Before we entered the digital era, these works were thought of as being "atomized."[13] At other moments, they were considered "serialized."

SHEAR
I think people saw the collages as fabric—as feminine and fabric, basically.

HUMPHRIES
Yes—think of a big basket full of fabric scraps and just grabbing from it. There is a randomness of aesthetic choice.

BIANCONI
It is also tied to the algorithmic. Certain choices must be made to make patterns in weaving.

HASKELL
Now we are almost at Anni Albers. But what I think is being discussed is an aspect of the vulnerability of the collages. In the moment of their making, one can see why it made sense for Ellsworth to keep them to himself, knowing that there are incredible ideas and potential in them, yet at the same time, recognizing that there was a risk in showing them too soon. When something becomes public, it changes. The artist loses an aspect of control. The work might lose associations you thought it had, and it might gain others.

HUMPHRIES
Ellsworth was an unknown young artist at the time, living in self-exile in Paris. He was trying to find his way. He was thinking about color—liberating color and creating a new basis for his relationship to it through experiment. He did this in a very rigorous way, following the arc to the end. These works became the springboard for all his subsequent work, and they also were his way of dealing with what had already happened. For this project, he was looking backward and looking forward. It was a formative point in his life as an artist.

But maybe the project was not meant to be seen in that way. To me, drawing is a private thing. It is a way of thinking. In the collages, you can see Ellsworth thinking. In a sense, the painting is the more public work. It is important for viewers to see the movement from drawing to painting, the private to the more public expression.

HIGGINS
I want to touch on the desire to name colors without necessarily categorizing them. It is a post-structural idea of language. When I say "orange," for example, each of us has a different hue of orange in mind. Yet, with these works, we can agree on a lot: we can see the system in place, we can see the anti-system in place, and we can see the colors. For the most part, we can agree on what each color is called, at least in general terms. At this moment, anarchism goes two ways; there is the branch of anarchism that wants to blow everything up, and then there is the naturalist side. For me, this line of thinking is in the direction of a kind of naturalism.

SHEAR
That is why I referred to Ellsworth as a "transcendental anarchist."

HUMPHRIES
It took thousands of years for civilization to arrive at these very colors.

HASKELL
I end up in a similar place, reflecting on all the centuries of composition and tradition that precede these non-compositional strategies. In the process of making these works, many profound questions must have been considered: What fundamental premises of art making am I willing to get rid of? What do I want to keep? What will I refuse to do? Ellsworth, through his process, was able to retain what was worth retaining and to set a path for new aesthetic experiences. The word I have for that is humanism. In these collages, we have art that speaks to the experience of being a human in Ellsworth's time.

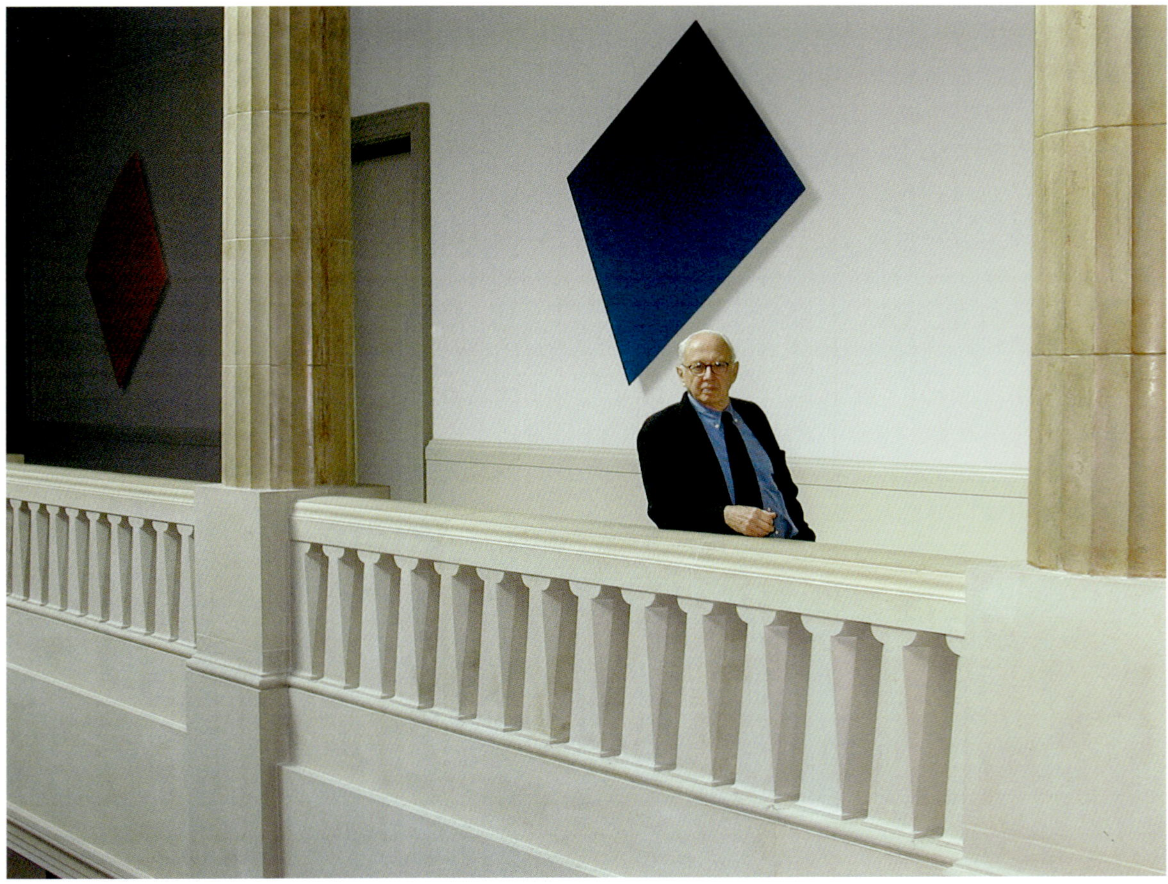

Fig. 17.   Ellsworth Kelly with two of *The Chicago Panels* (1989–99),
the Art Institute of Chicago, August 1999.

HUMPHRIES
The destruction of Europe provided an opportunity to rebuild. But how was that going to be done? These works represent one way to go about rebuilding: color and painting.

BIANCONI
That is where the publicness of these works comes from, and the importance of Ellsworth being in private to exercise the experimentation. That dialectic is really strong.

HIGGINS
We should talk a bit about Byzantium.

HASKELL
I do feel that there is something Byzantine in these works. Maybe that is another reason that Ellsworth held them back, because it would have been easy for people to say, "Oh, it's mosaic. I've seen something like this before."

But beyond the superficial association with tesserae, Byzantine art does offer a powerful point of comparison. You can hold each of the mosaic stones; you can know them as things in the world; and you can simultaneously see a mosaic as a sacred image. We could debate whether the work is more about its material or its image, but in the mysterious interworking

of the two, it is a little bit like transcendentalism.

HUMPHRIES
There is a paint by numbers-ness to mosaic and a sense that almost anyone, even a child, can do it. The tactility of the pieces and the predetermined structure are appealing.

HIGGINS
Yet the pieces are always a little off. They do not quite lie flat.

HUMPHRIES
Right, and that is okay. There is an allowance for that.

SHEAR
As I stand here among these collages, I can't help but think of Ellsworth's commission, the only building that he designed, entitled *Austin* (2015; Blanton Museum of Art, Austin). He picked the colors of its square glass windows, and he used squares for the *Stations of the Cross*, the fourteen marble panels that fill the interior of the space. Ellsworth was an atheist, but he was inspired by Christian iconography and the great churches he visited throughout Europe.

When you see the beautiful spectrum of colors of *Austin* shining with light, so alive, it becomes a culmination of Ellsworth's life and work.

1   John Coplans, "The Earlier Work of Ellsworth Kelly," *Artforum* 7, no. 10 (Summer 1969): 48–55, https://www.artforum.com/features/the-earlier-work-of-ellsworth-kelly-210775.
2   See, for example, Diane Waldman, introduction to *Ellsworth Kelly: Drawings, Collages, Prints* (Greenwich, CT: New York Graphic Society, 1971), 18.
3   See, for example, Coplans, "Earlier Work," 52, 54; John Coplans, *Ellsworth Kelly* (New York: H. N. Abrams, [1972 or 1973]), 15–16, 45–46, 53, 57–58; and E. C. Goossen, *Ellsworth Kelly*, exh. cat. (New York: Museum of Modern Art, 1973), 19, 32, 46, 76.
4   For Gadamer's concept of the horizon as a hermeneutic ontology, see Hans-Georg Gadamer, *Truth and Method* (1960; London: Continuum, 1975).
5   Thomas B. Hess, "Reinhardt: The Position and Perils of Purity," review of Ad Reinhardt's show at the Betty Parsons Gallery, New York, November 16–December 5, 1953. *ARTnews* 52, no. 8 (December 1953): 26–27.
6   Yve-Alain Bois, "Ellsworth Kelly in France: Anti-Composition in Its Many Guises," in Yve-Alain Bois, Jack Cowart, and Alfred Pacquement, *Ellsworth Kelly: The Years in France, 1948–1954*, exh. cat. (Washington, DC: National Gallery of Art, 1992), 9–36, 27 ("interstitial surface").
7   Duchamp worked on the *Rotoreliefs* series from 1935 to 1953; he first printed a portion of the works in 1953.
8   Ellsworth Kelly, "Ellsworth Kelly: Talking to America's Most Colorful Artist," interview by Paul Taylor, *Interview* 21, no. 6 (June 1991), cited in Diane Waldman, ed., *Ellsworth Kelly: A Retrospective*, exh. cat. (New York: Guggenheim Museum, 1996), 41.
9   On Ellsworth Kelly's service in US military deception groups, see Philip Gerard, *The Secret Soldiers: The Story of World War II's Heroic Army of Deception* (New York: Dutton, 2002), 63.
10   Brecht's essay was later published as a book: George Brecht, *Chance-Imagery* (New York: Something Else Press, 1966).
11   Ambrogio Lorenzetti (Italian, active 1317–48), *Virgin and Child*, late 1330s–early 1340s, Museum of Fine Arts, Boston, acc. no. 39.536.
12   Howard Singerman, "Noncompositional Effects, or the Process of Painting in 1970," *Oxford Art Journal* 26, no. 1 (2003): 125–50, http://www.jstor.org/stable/3600449.
13   Coplans, "Earlier Work," 51.

**All works are by Ellsworth Kelly
(American, 1923–2015).**

Plates

Ellsworth Kelly. *Spectrum Colors Arranged by Chance I*, 1951. Collage on paper; 50 × 99.7 cm (19¹¹/₁₆ × 39¼ in.). Philadelphia Museum of Art, purchased with funds contributed by C. K. Williams, II (by exchange), 2007-30-3.

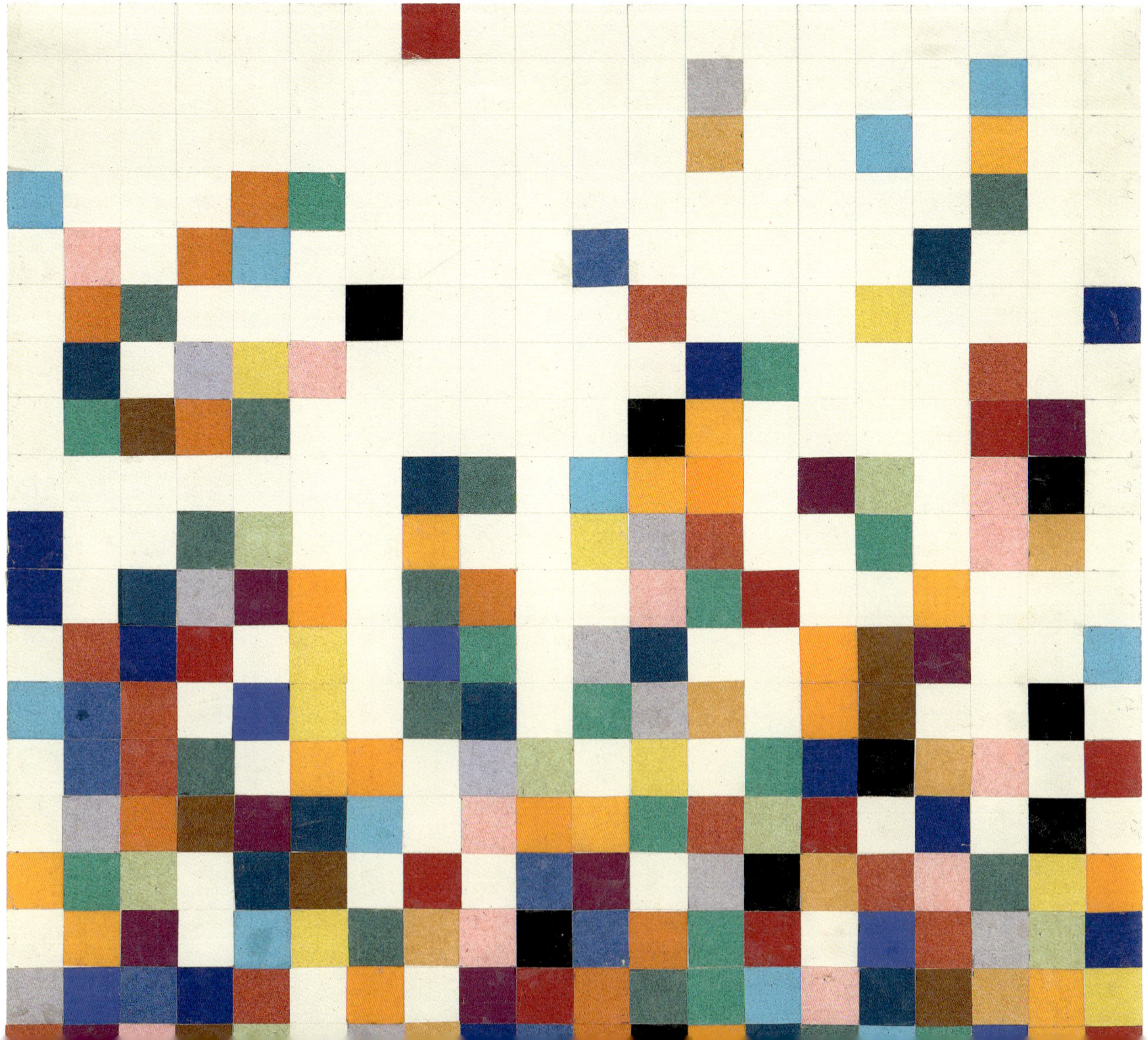

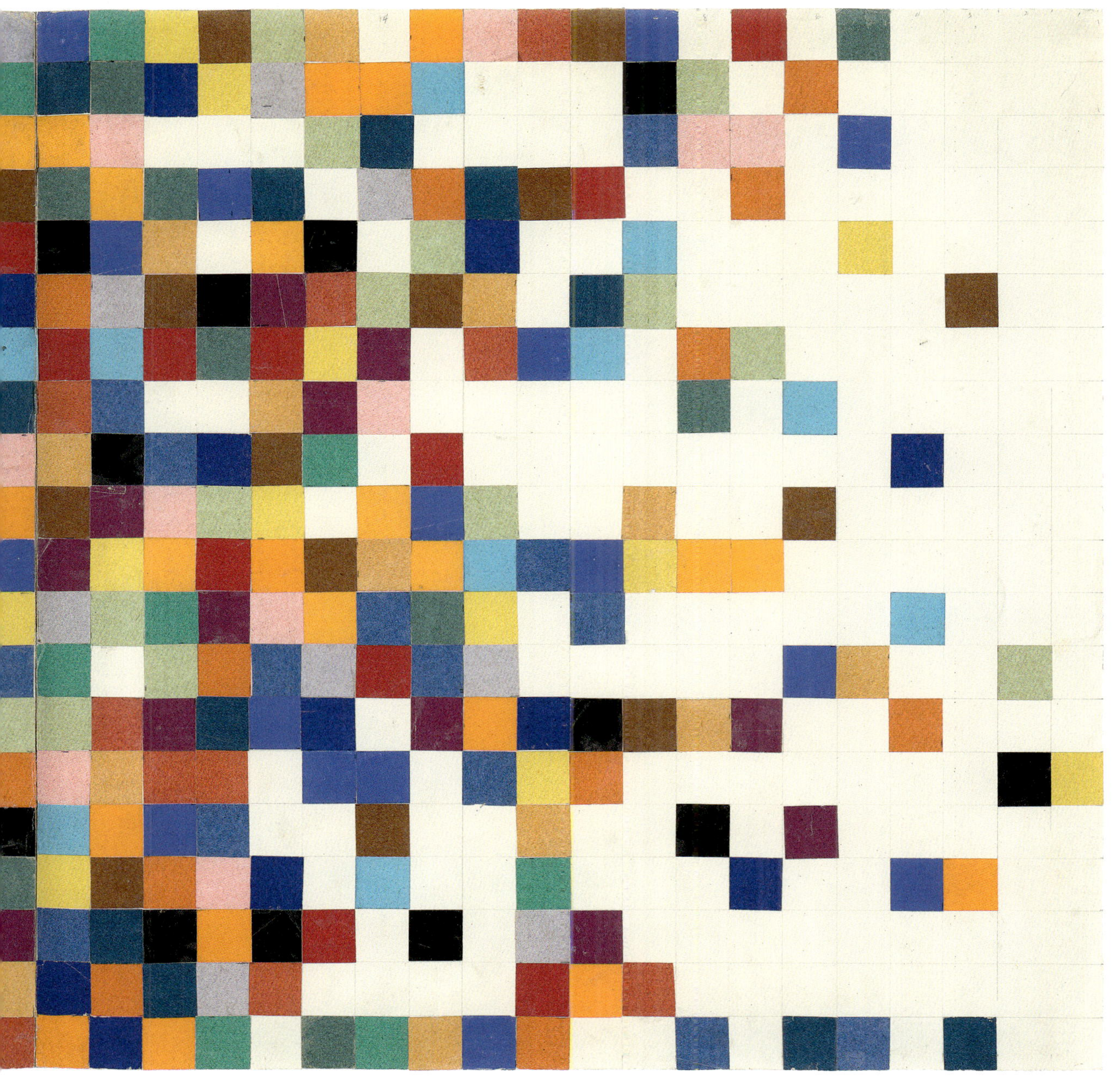

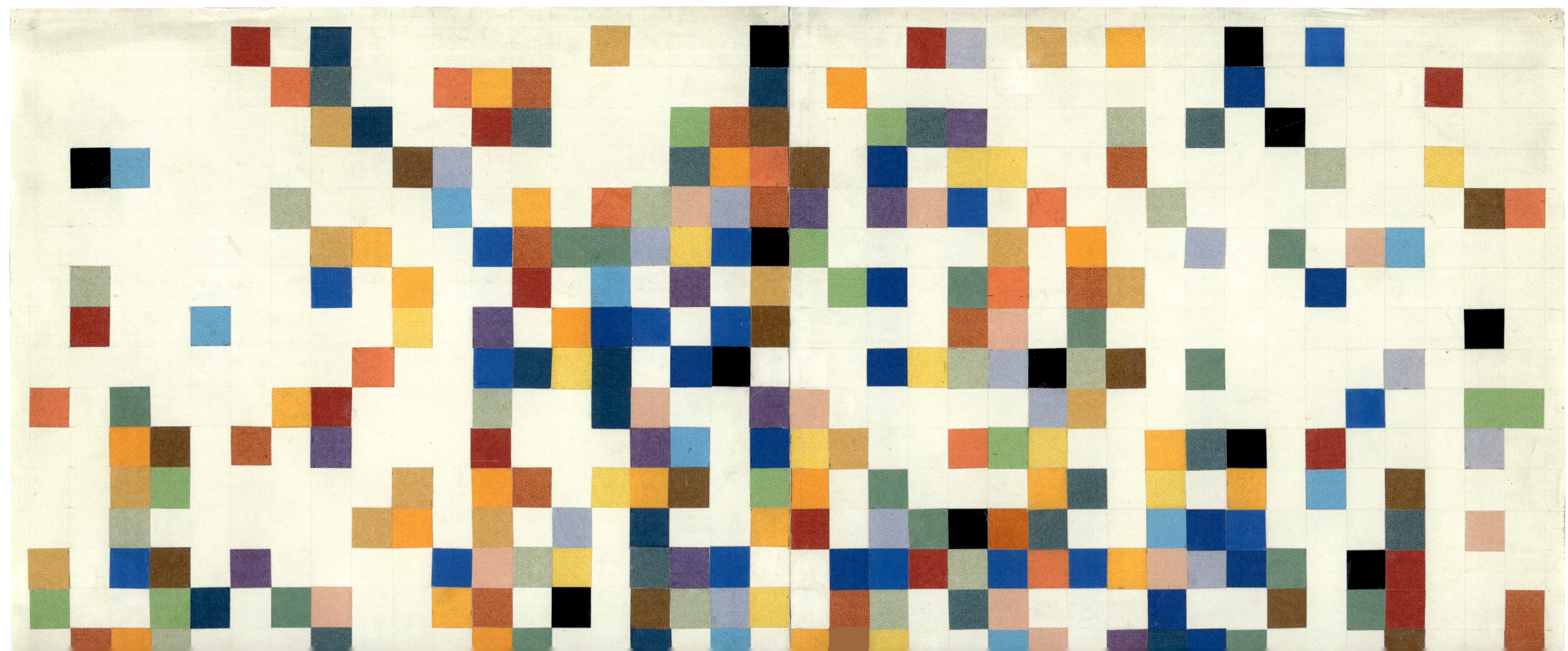

Ellsworth Kelly. *Spectrum Colors Arranged by Chance II*, 1951. Collage on paper; 97.2 × 97.2 cm (38¼ × 38¼ in.). The Museum of Modern Art, New York, purchased with funds provided by Jo Carole and Ronald S. Lauder, 500.1997.

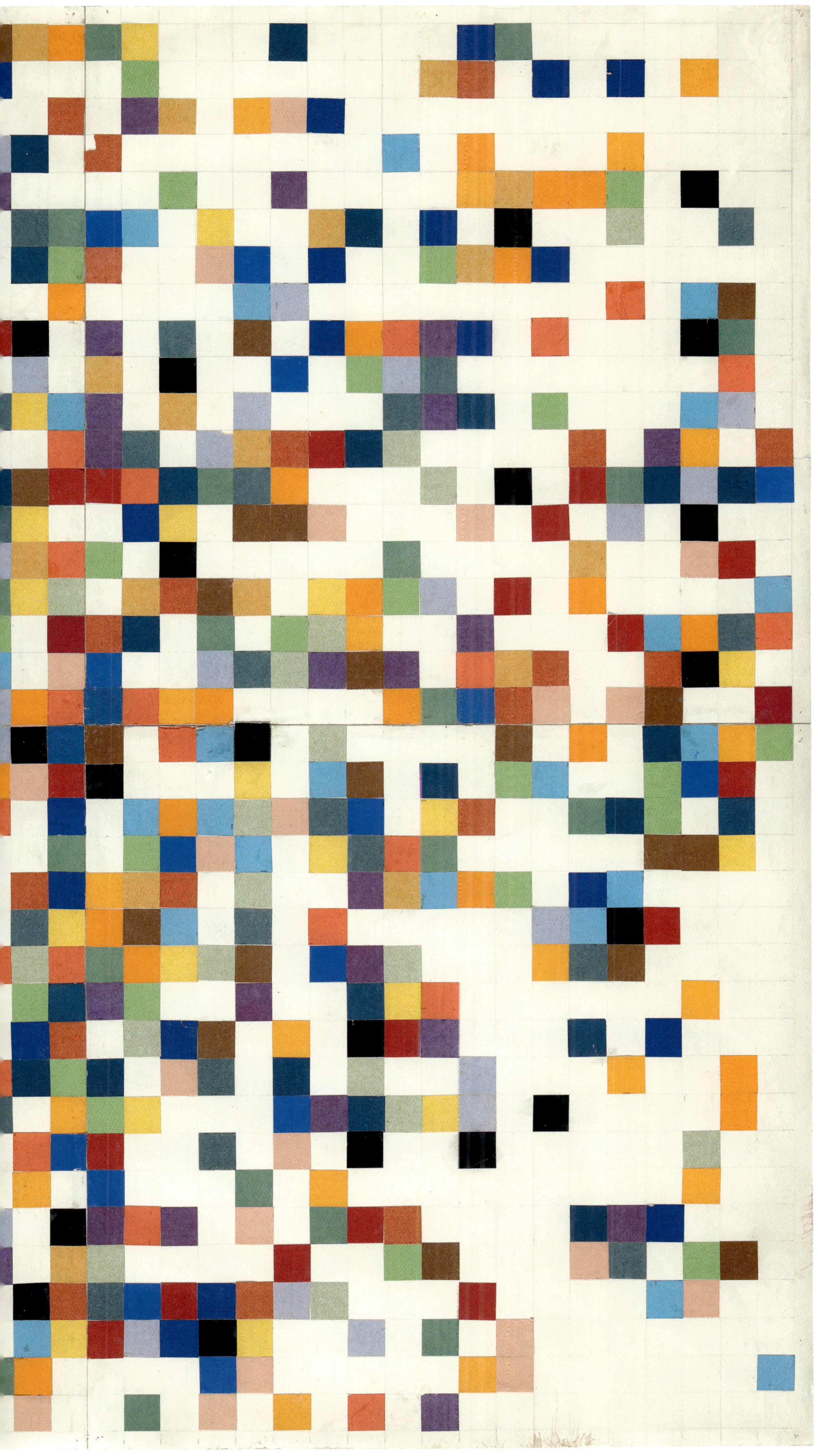

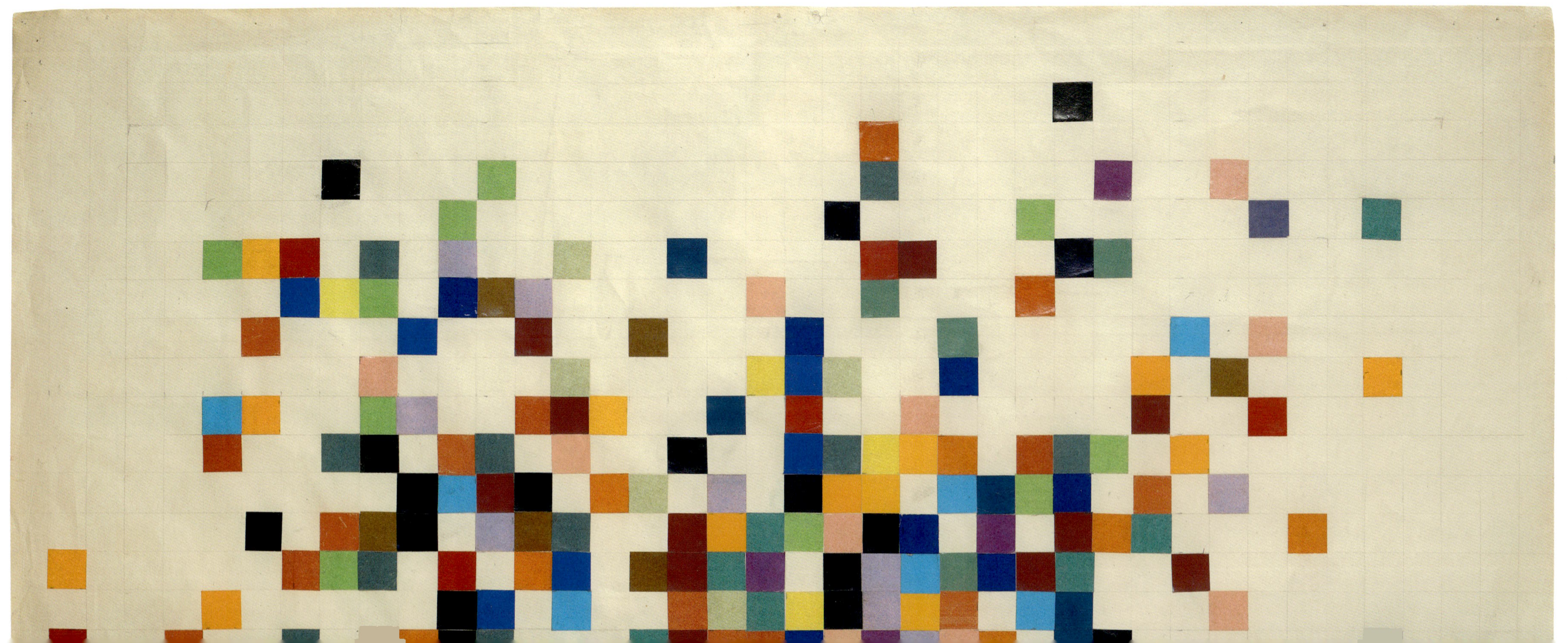

Ellsworth Kelly. *Spectrum Colors Arranged by Chance III,* 1951. Collage on paper; 99.1 × 99.1 cm (39 × 39 in.). Kravis Collection.

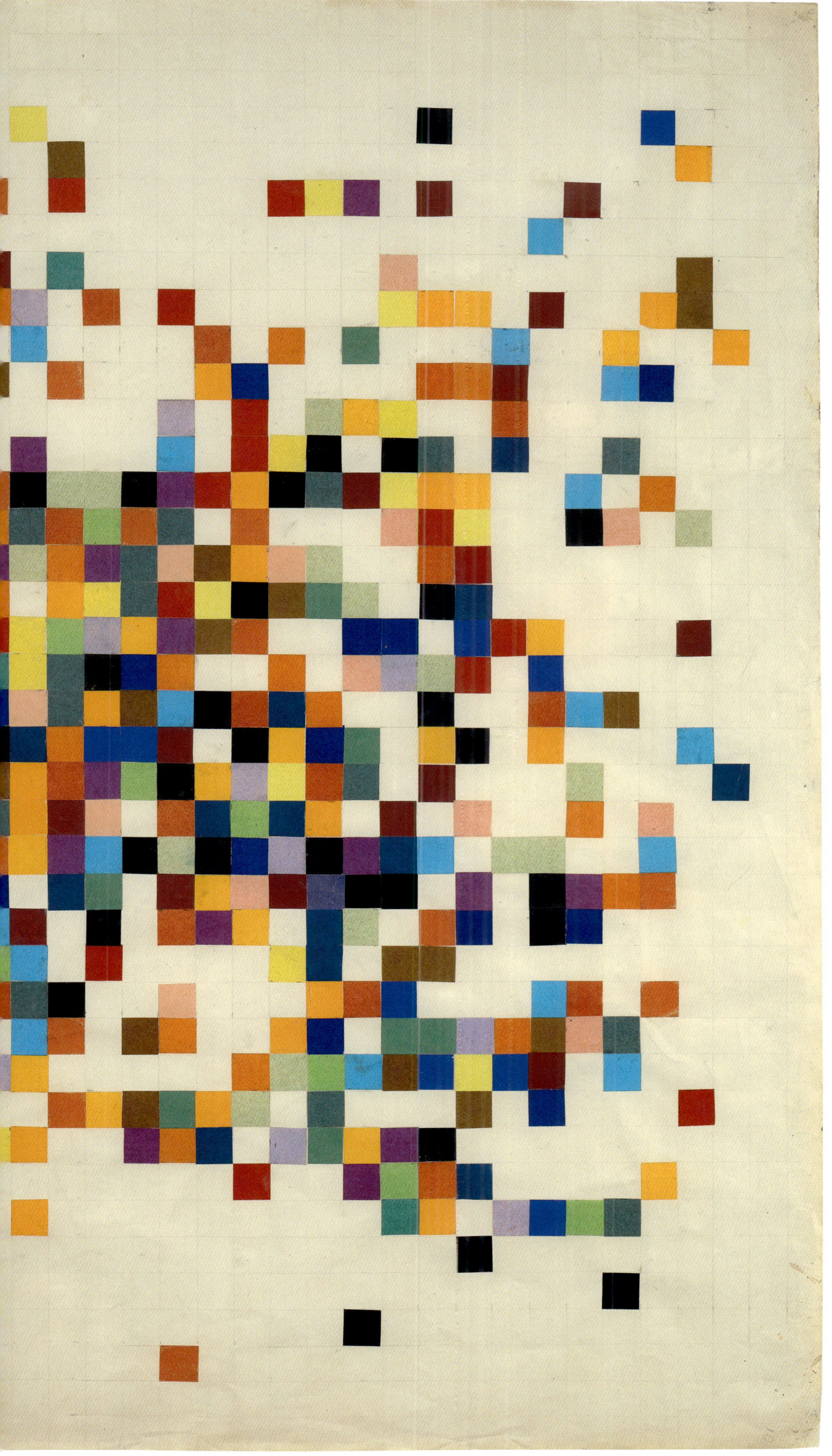

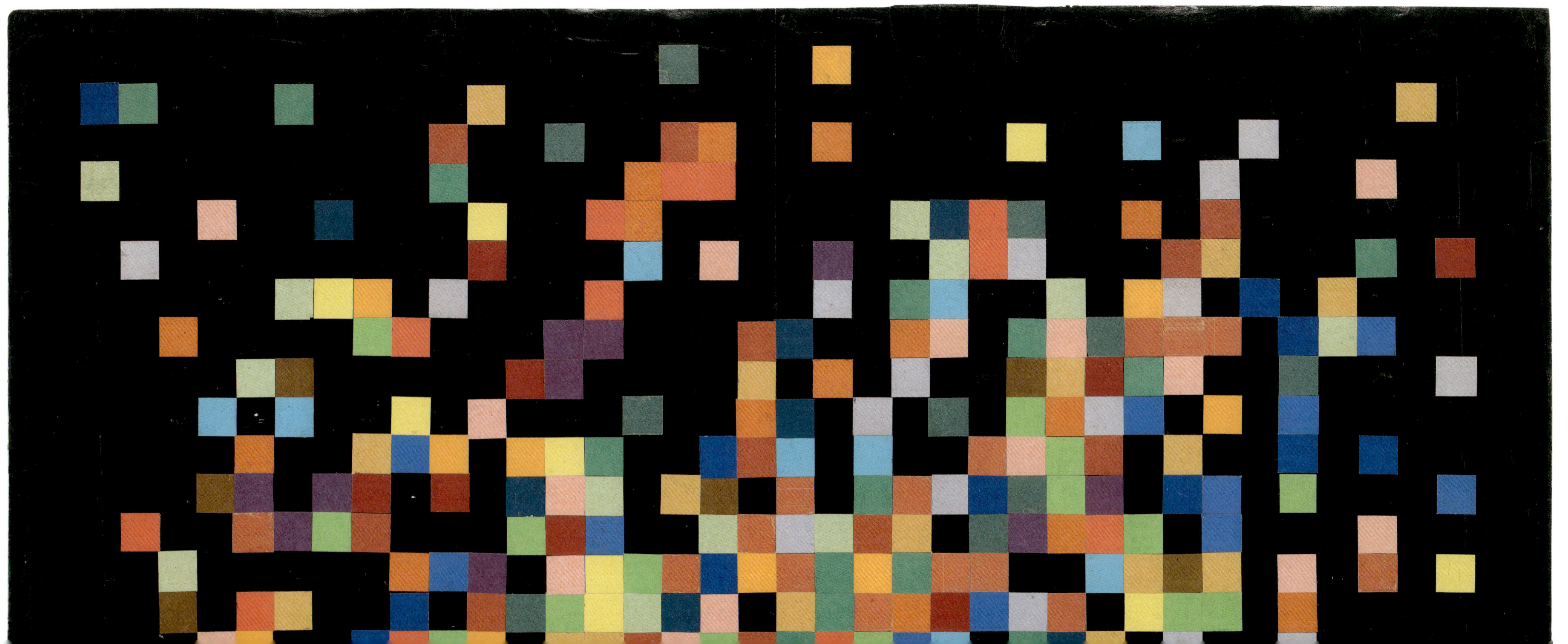

Ellsworth Kelly. *Spectrum Colors Arranged by Chance IV*, 1951. Collage on paper; 99.6 × 99.5 cm (39¼ × 39³⁄₁₆ in.). The Art Institute of Chicago, Margaret Fisher Endowment, 2001.139.

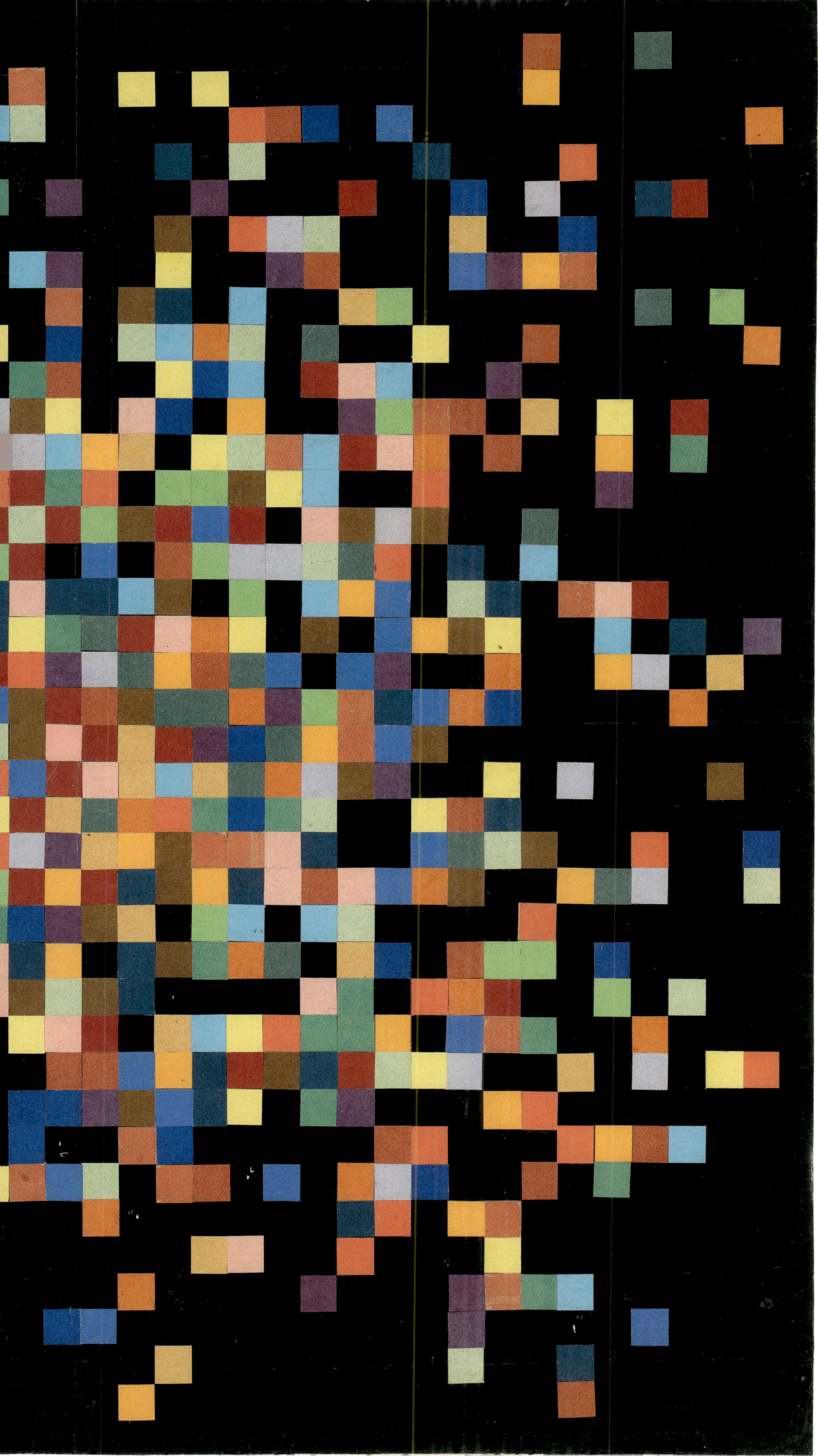

Ellsworth Kelly. *Spectrum Colors Arranged by Chance V*, 1951. Collage on paper; 99.1 × 99.1 cm (39 × 39 in.). Aaron I. Fleischman.

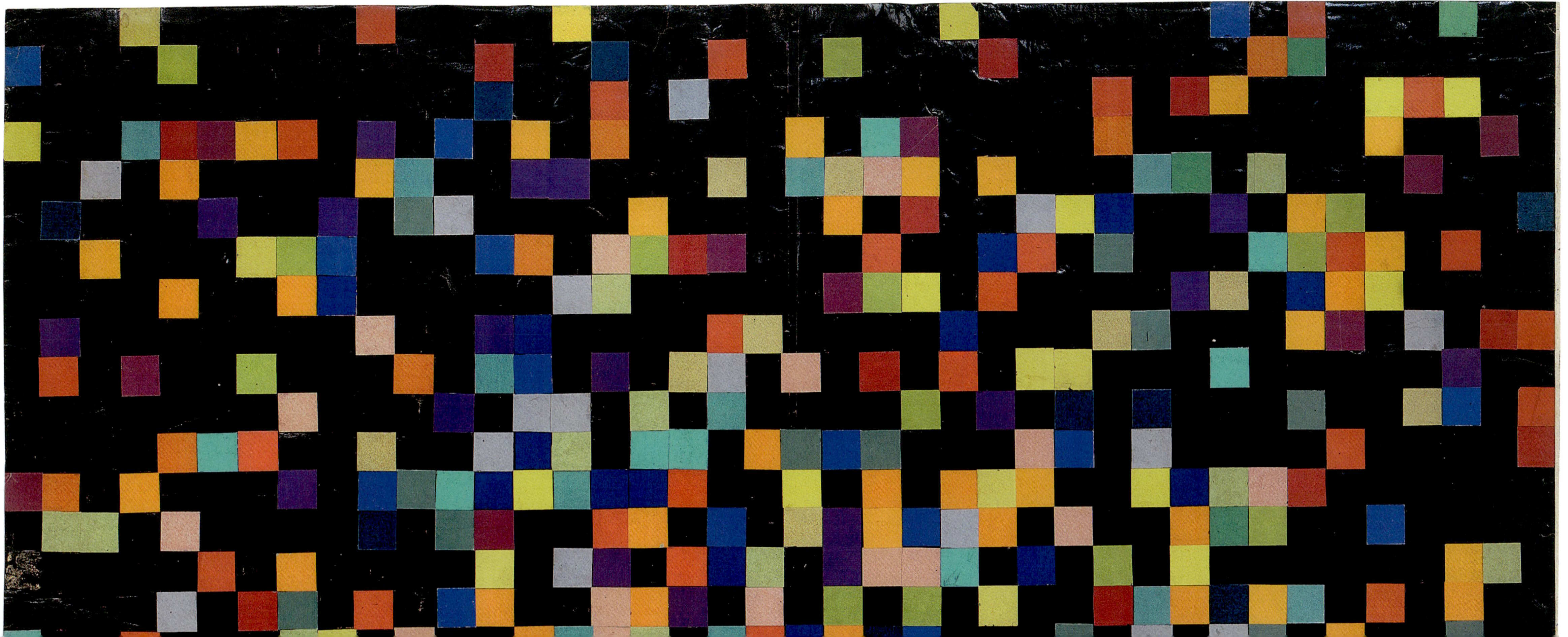

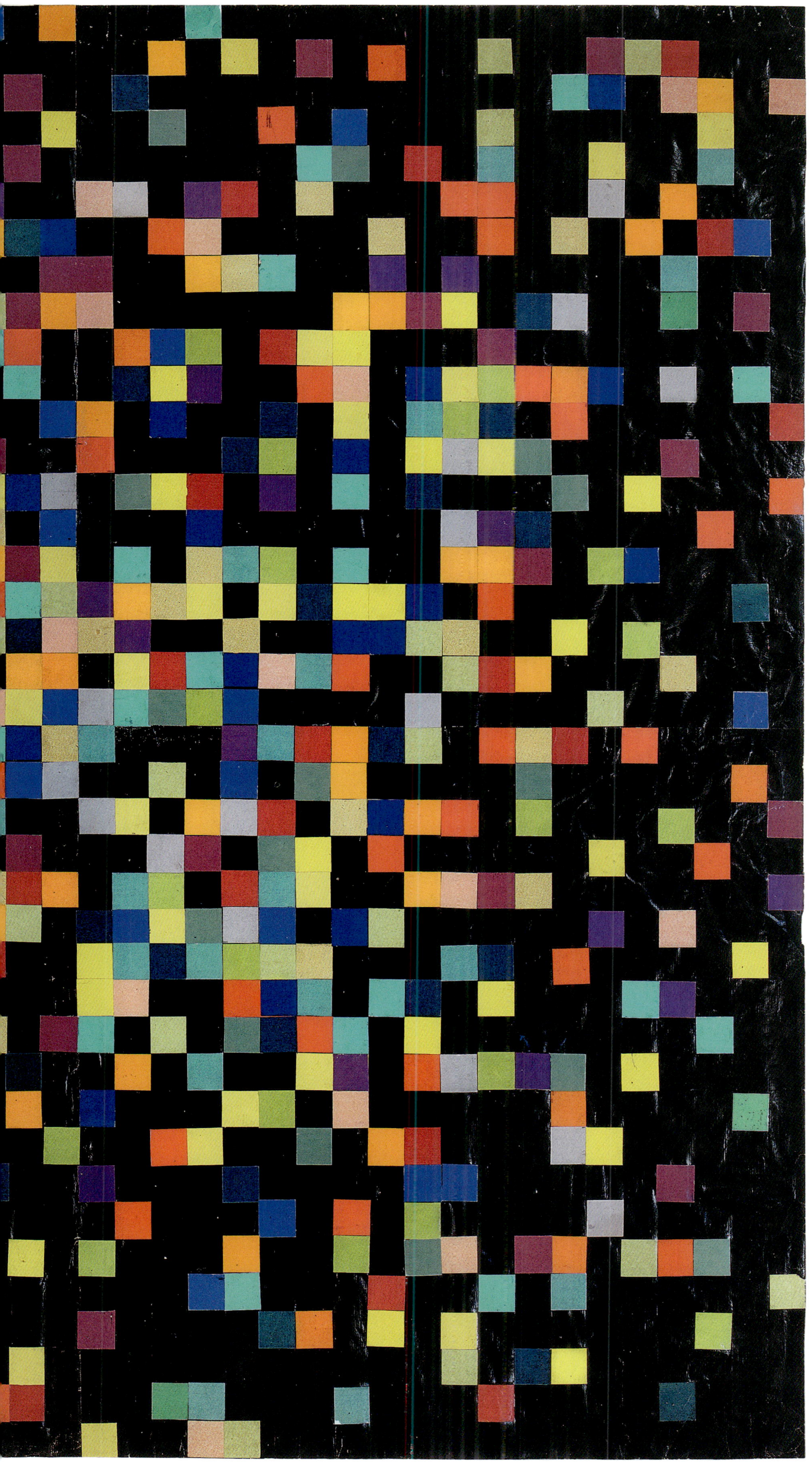

Ellsworth Kelly. *Spectrum Colors Arranged by Chance VI*, 1951. Collage on paper; 93.4 × 93.4 cm (36¾ × 36¾ in.). The Museum of Modern Art, New York, purchased with funds provided by The Edward John Noble Foundation, The Herbert and Nanette Rothschild Fund, and Mrs. Pierre Matisse, 243.2000.

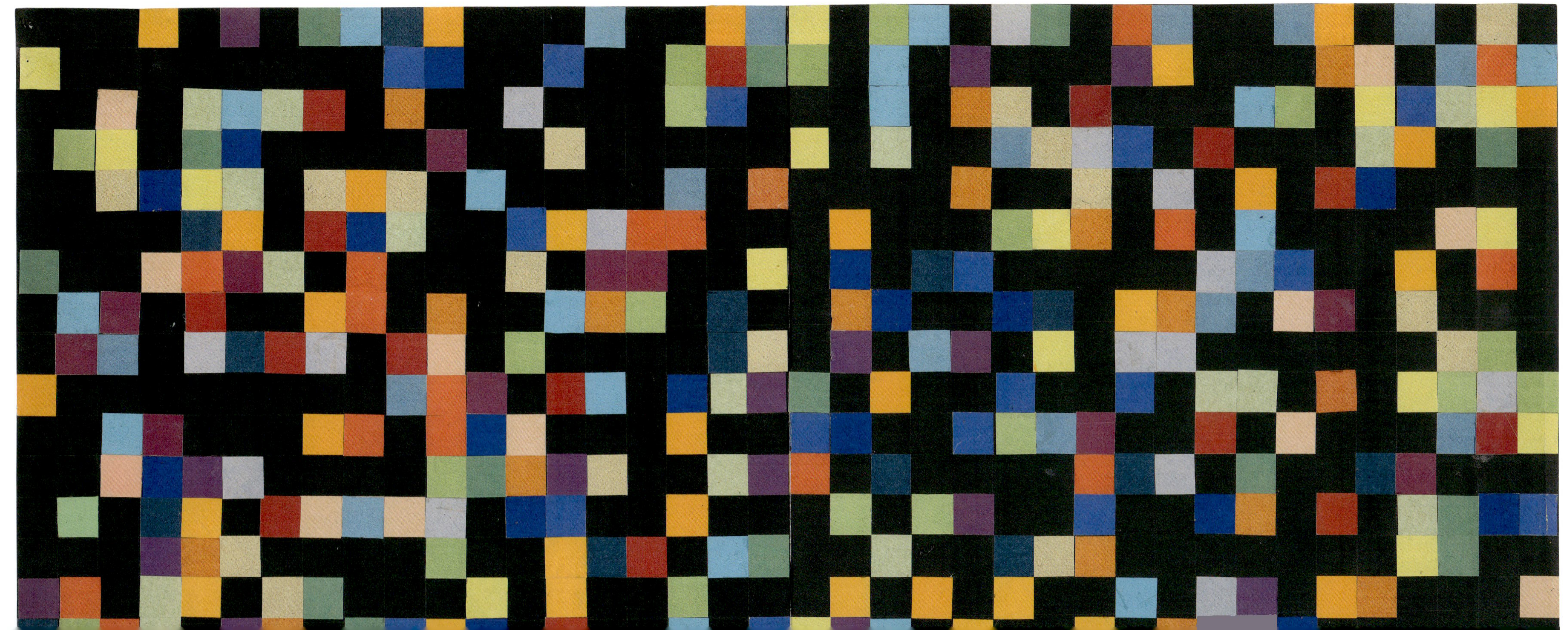

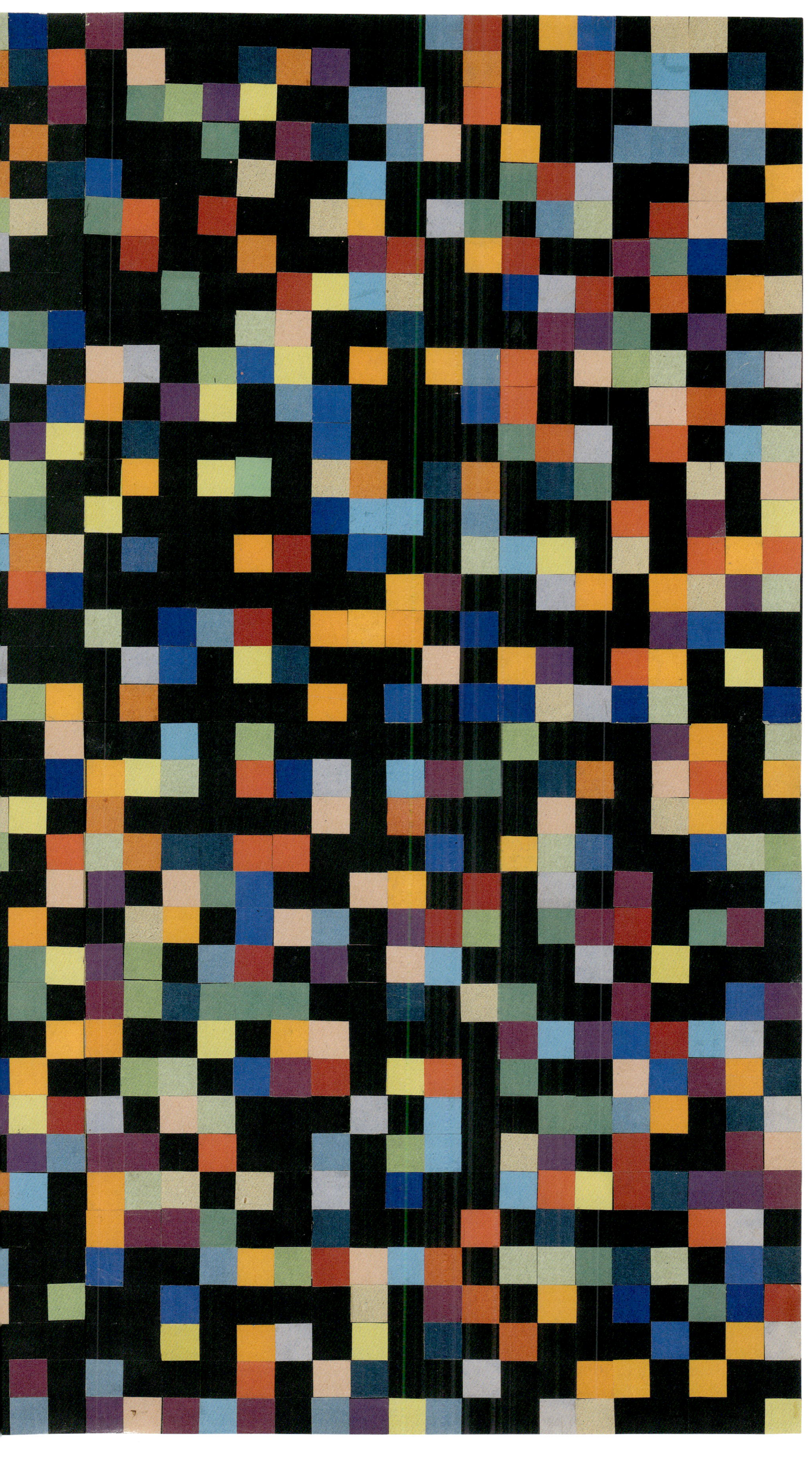

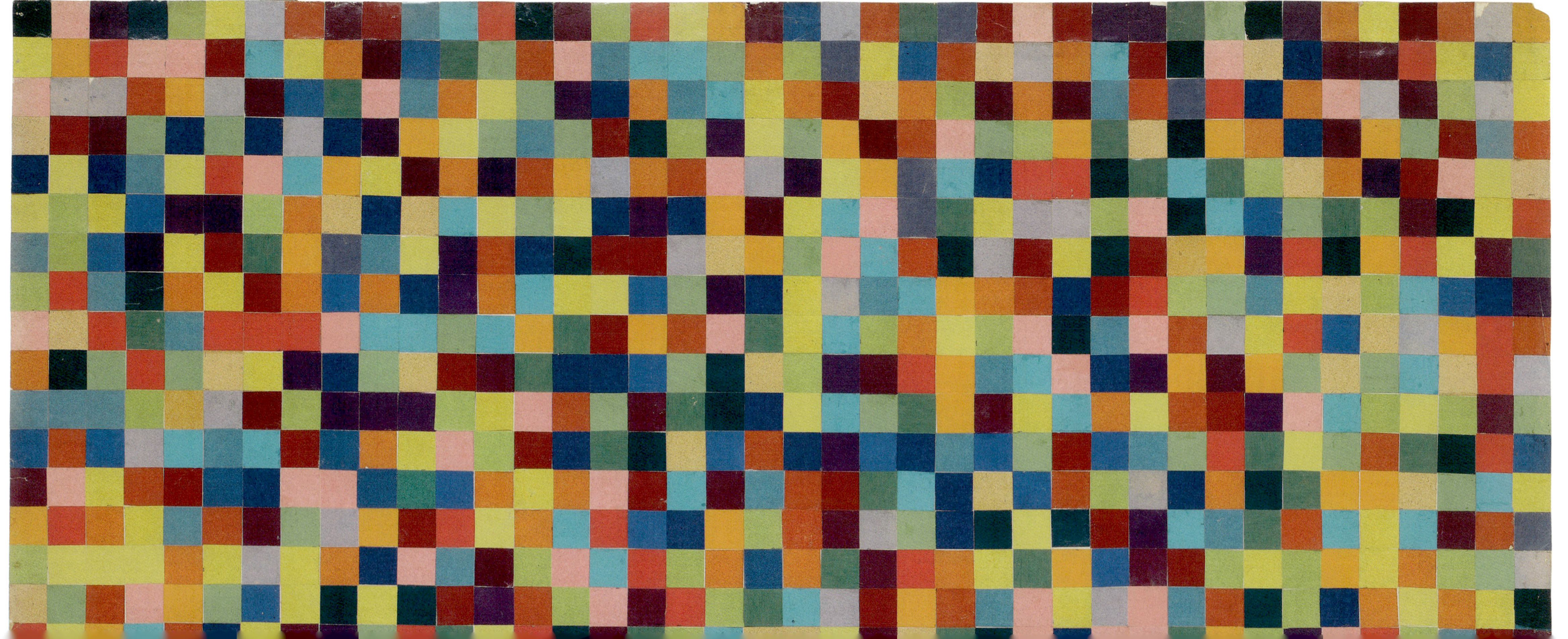

Ellsworth Kelly. *Spectrum Colors Arranged by Chance VII*, 1951. Collage on paper; 99 × 100 cm (39 × 39⅜ in.). Glenstone Museum, Potomac, Maryland.

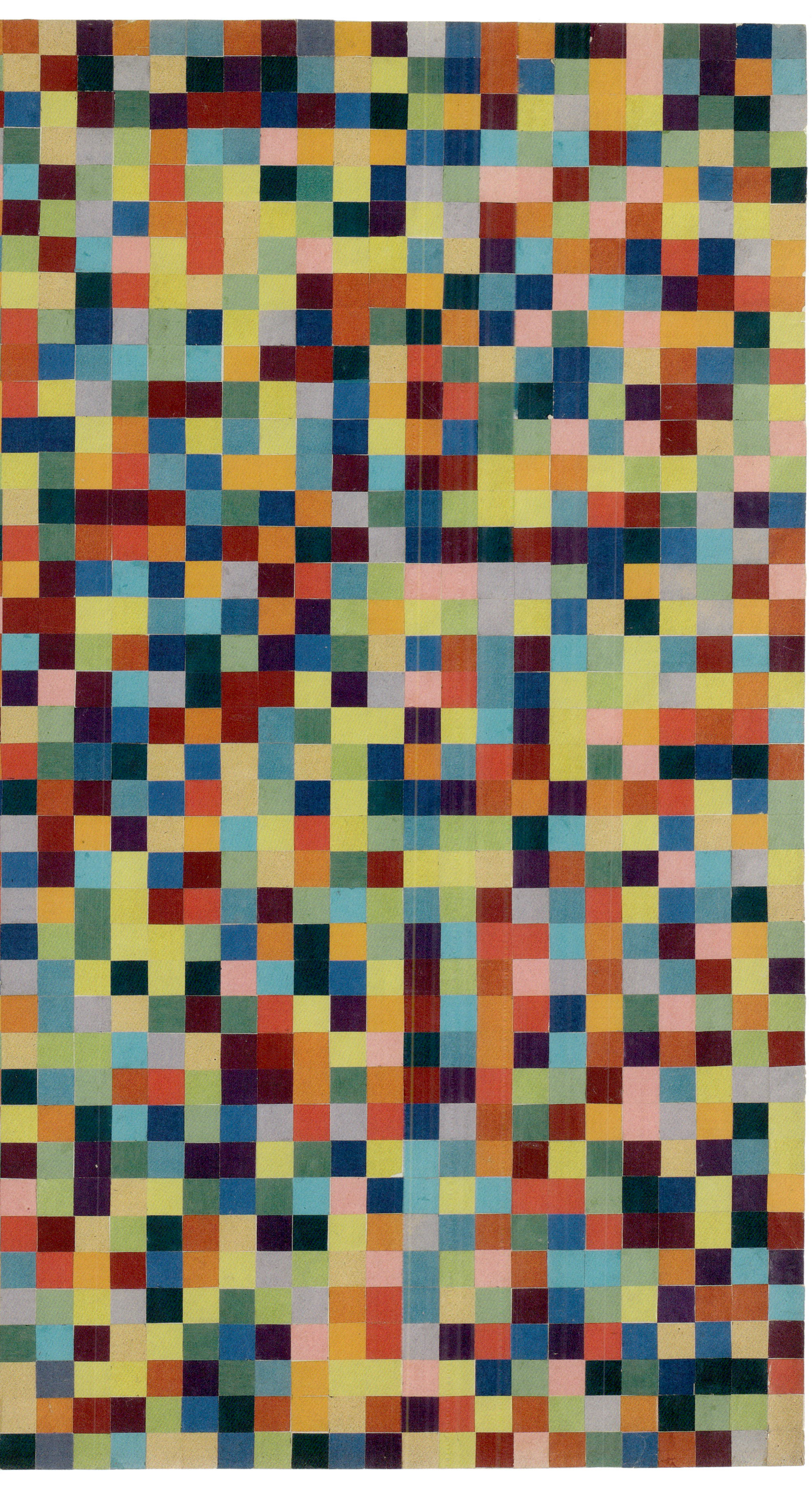

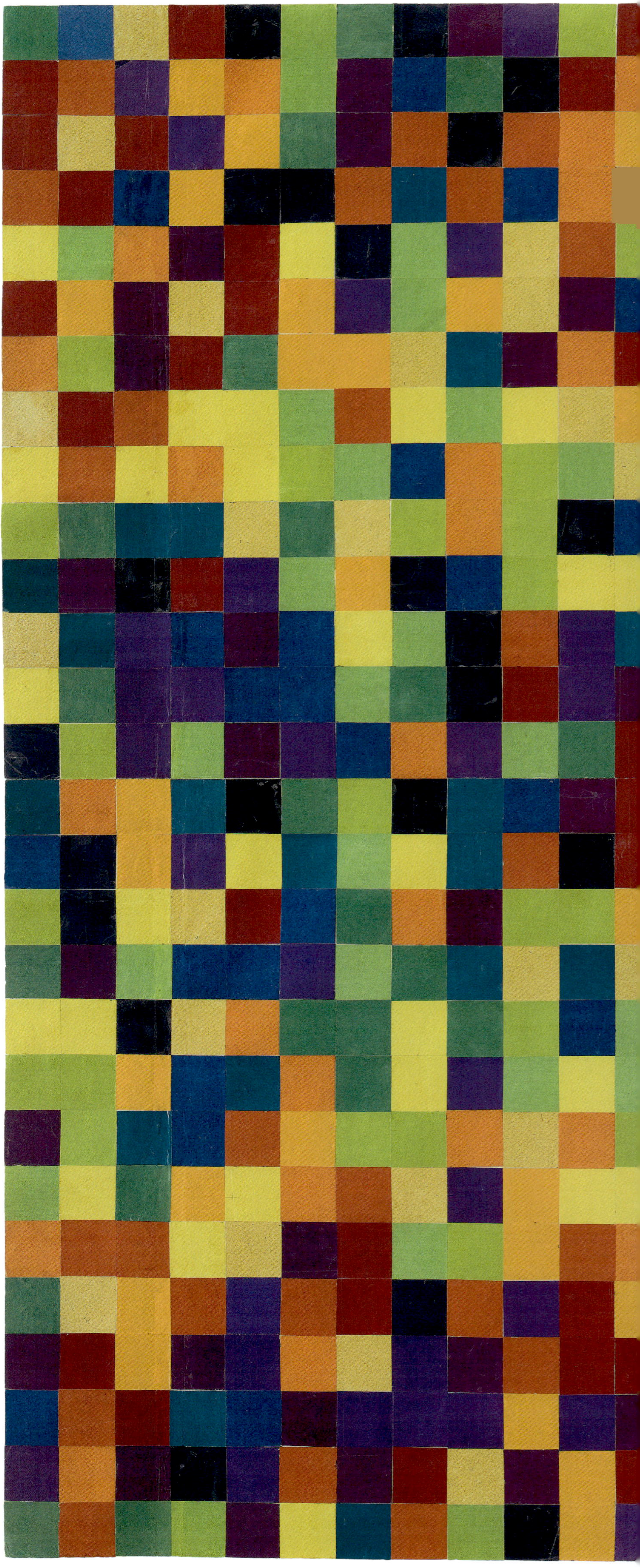

Ellsworth Kelly. *Spectrum Colors Arranged by Chance VIII*, 1951. Collage on paper; 111.8 × 111.8 cm (44 × 44 in.). Private collection.

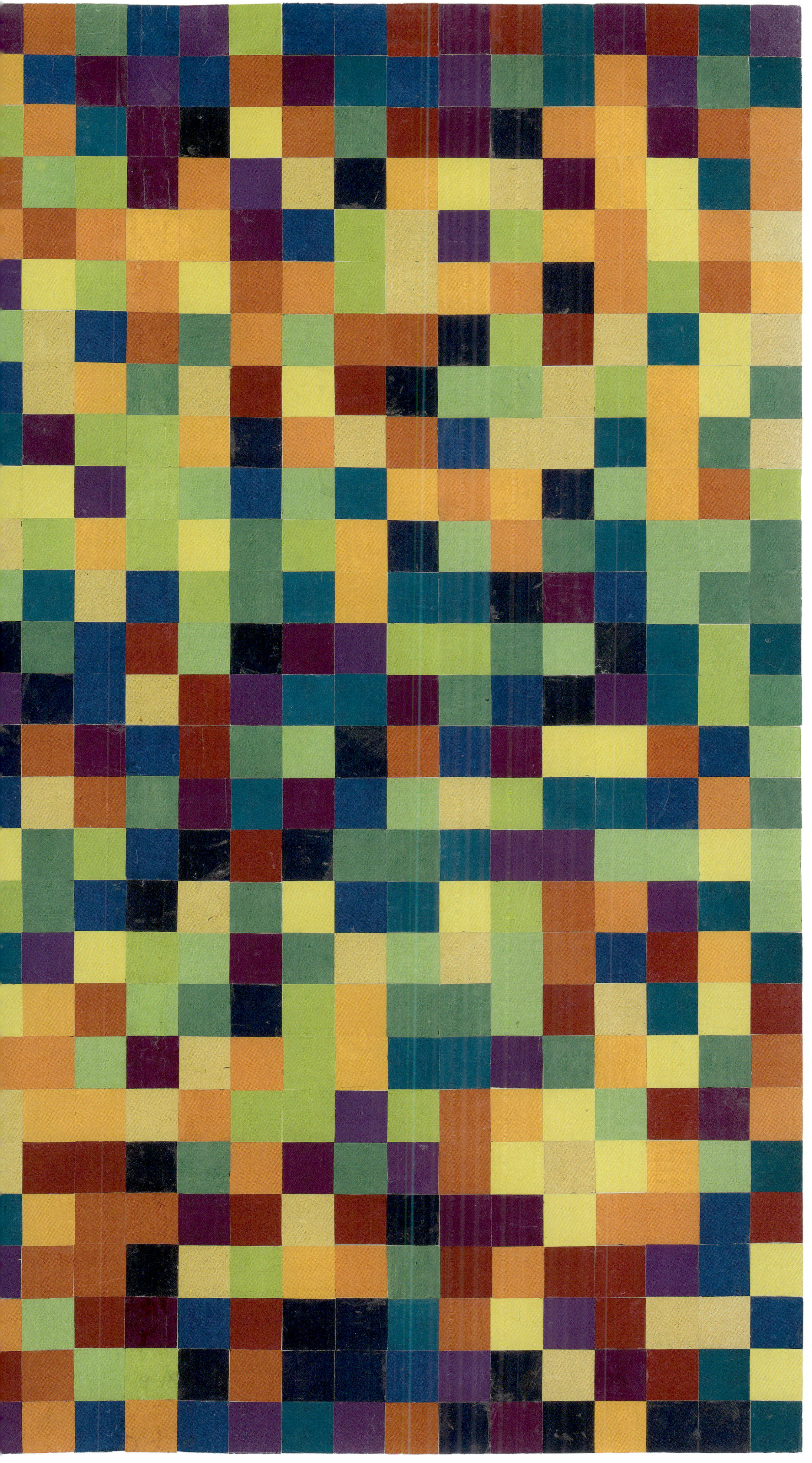

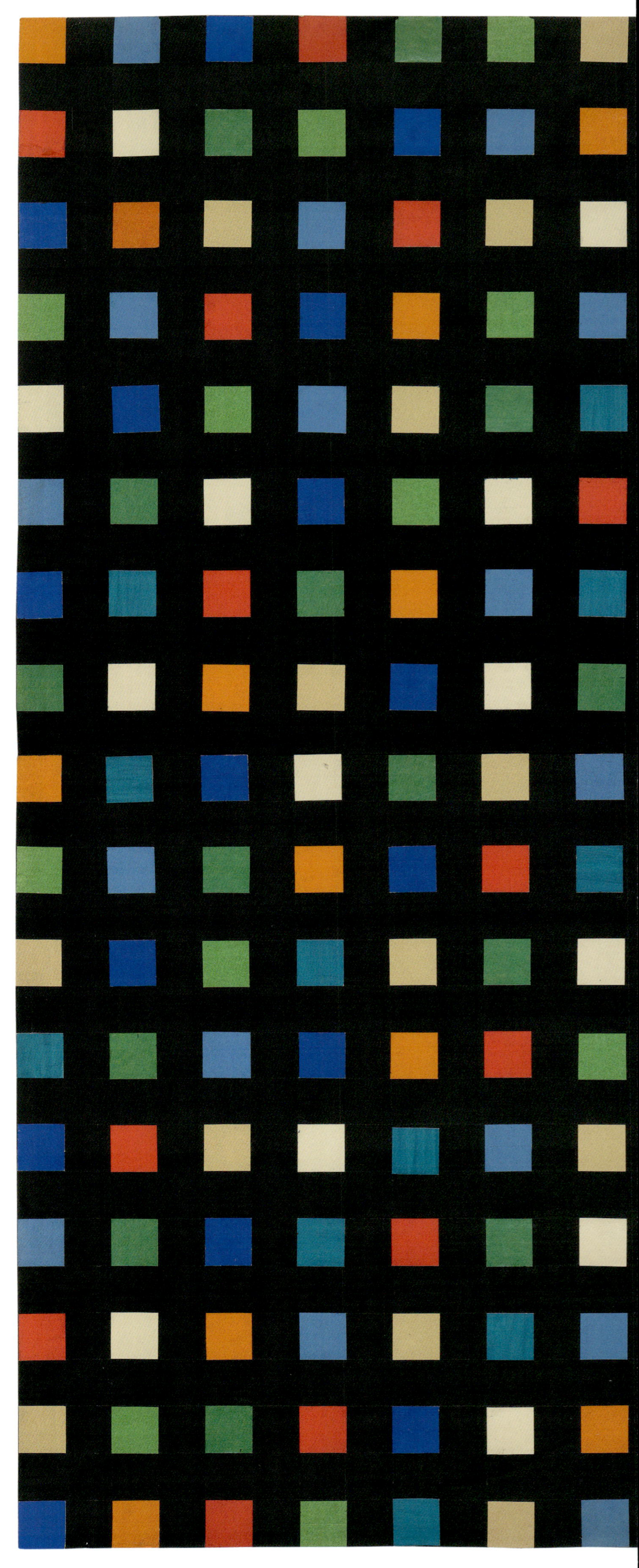

Ellsworth Kelly. *Spectrum Colors Arranged by Chance IX,* 1953. Collage on paper; 97.2 × 97.2 cm (38¹/₄ × 38¹/₄ in.). The Art Institute of Chicago, gift of Jack Shear in honor of the Ellsworth Kelly Centennial, 2024.801.

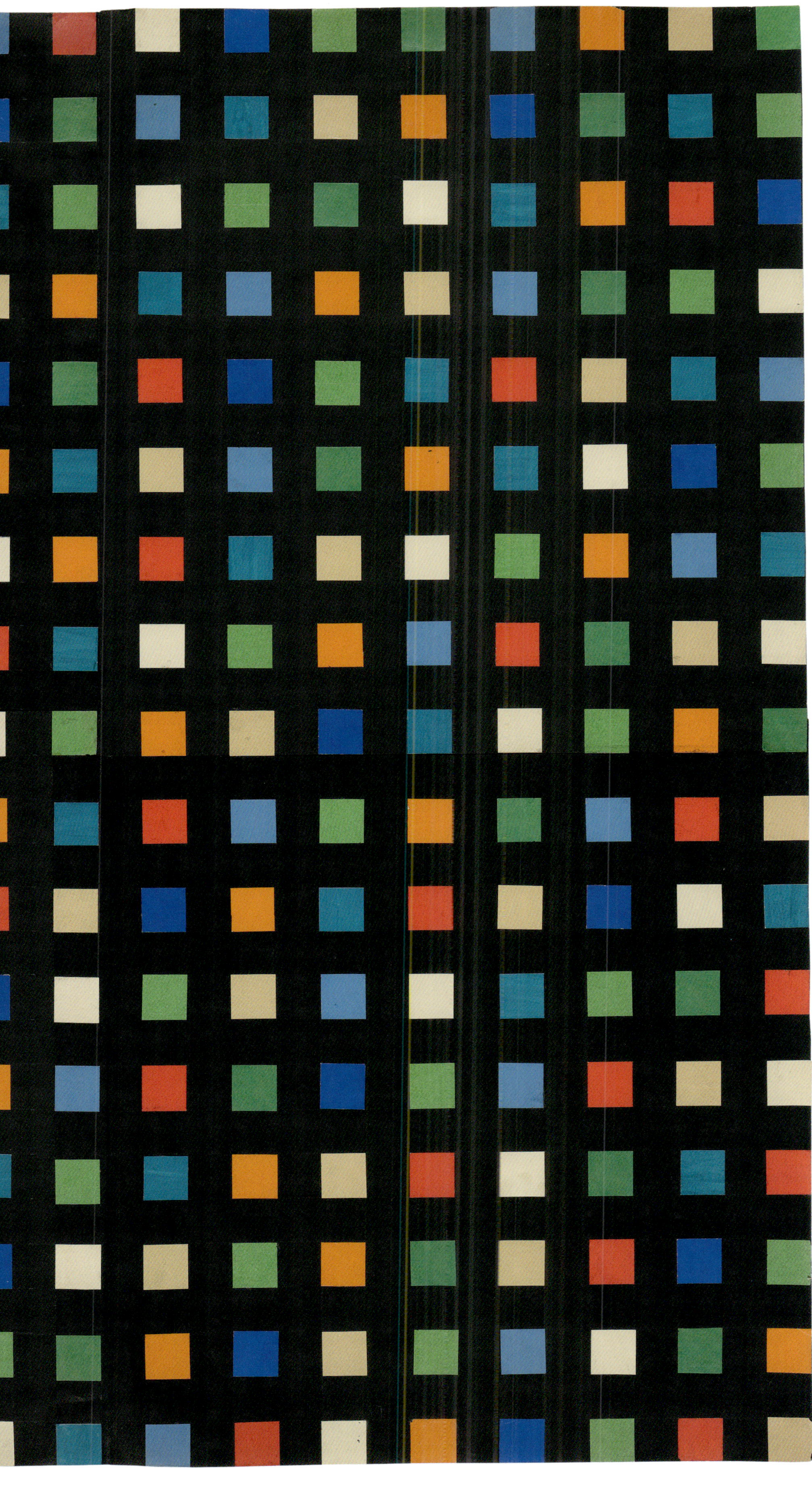

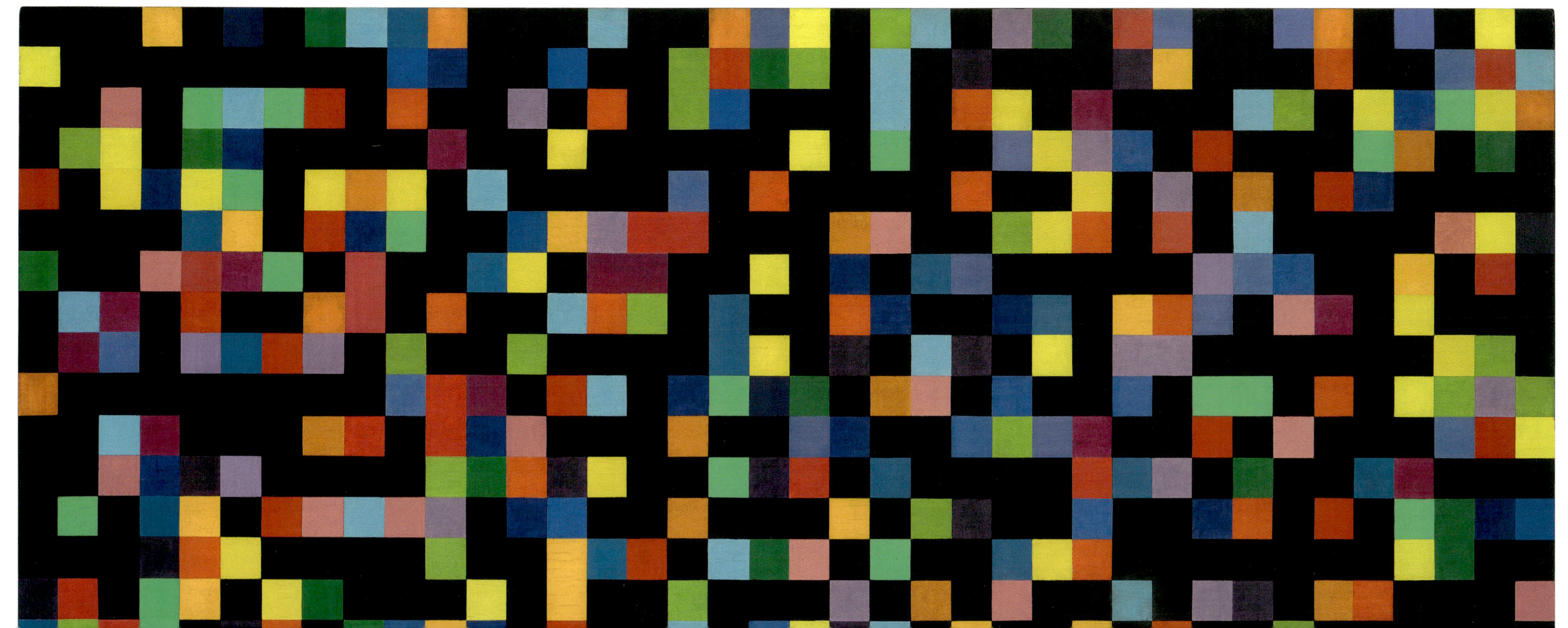

Ellsworth Kelly. *Spectrum Colors Arranged by Chance*, 1953. Oil on wood; 152.4 × 152.4 cm (60 × 60 in.). San Francisco Museum of Modern Art, the Doris and Donald Fisher Collection at the San Francisco Museum of Modern Art, and promised gift of Helen and Charles Schwab.

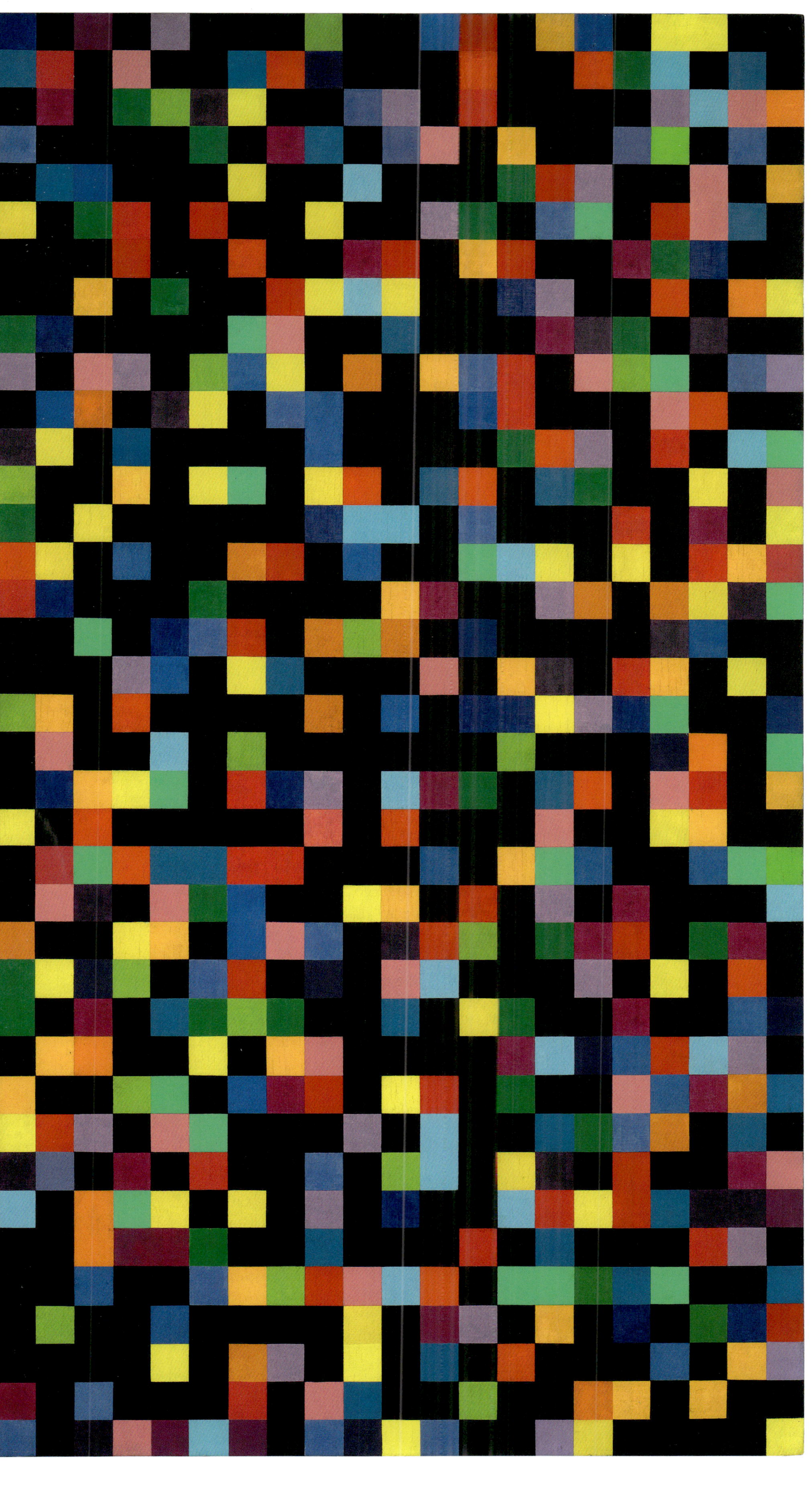

Installation Views

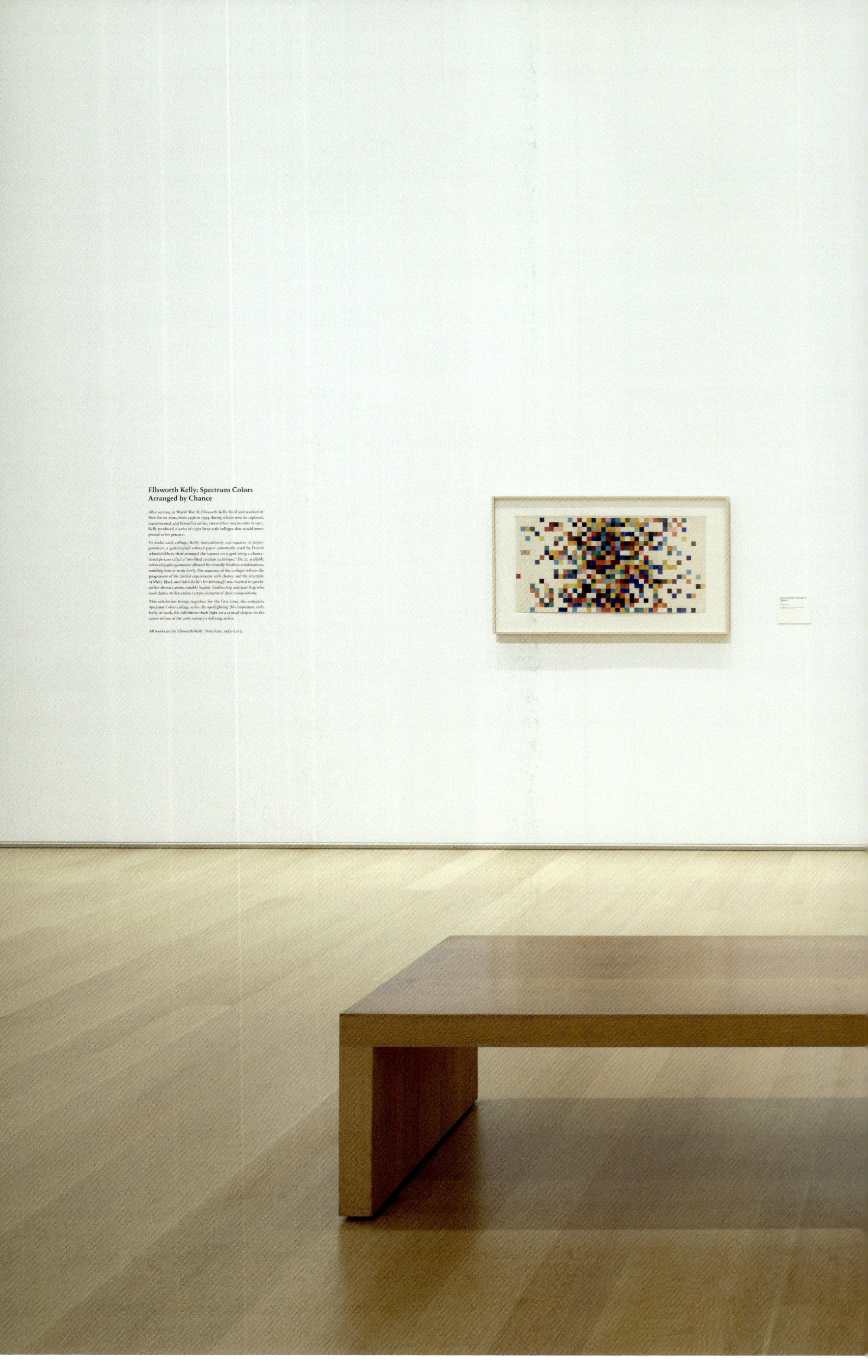

Ellsworth Kelly: Spectrum Colors
Arranged by Chance

After serving in World War II, Ellsworth Kelly lived and worked in Paris for six years, from 1948 to 1954, during which time he explored, experimented, and honed his artistic vision. Over two months in 1951, Kelly produced a series of eight large-scale collages that would prove pivotal to his practice.

To make each collage, Kelly meticulously cut squares of papier gommette, a gum-backed colored paper commonly used by French schoolchildren, then arranged the squares on a grid using a chance-based process called a "modified random technique." The 20 available colors of papier gommette allowed for virtually limitless combinations, enabling him to work freely. The sequence of the collages reflects the progression of his careful experiments with chance and the interplay of white, black, and color. Kelly's breakthrough was inspired in part by earlier abstract artists, notably Sophie Taeuber-Arp and Jean Arp, who used chance to determine certain elements of their compositions.

This exhibition brings together, for the first time, the complete Spectrum Colors collage series. By spotlighting this important early body of work, the exhibition sheds light on a critical chapter in the career of one of the 20th century's defining artists.

All works are by Ellsworth Kelly (American, 1923–2015).

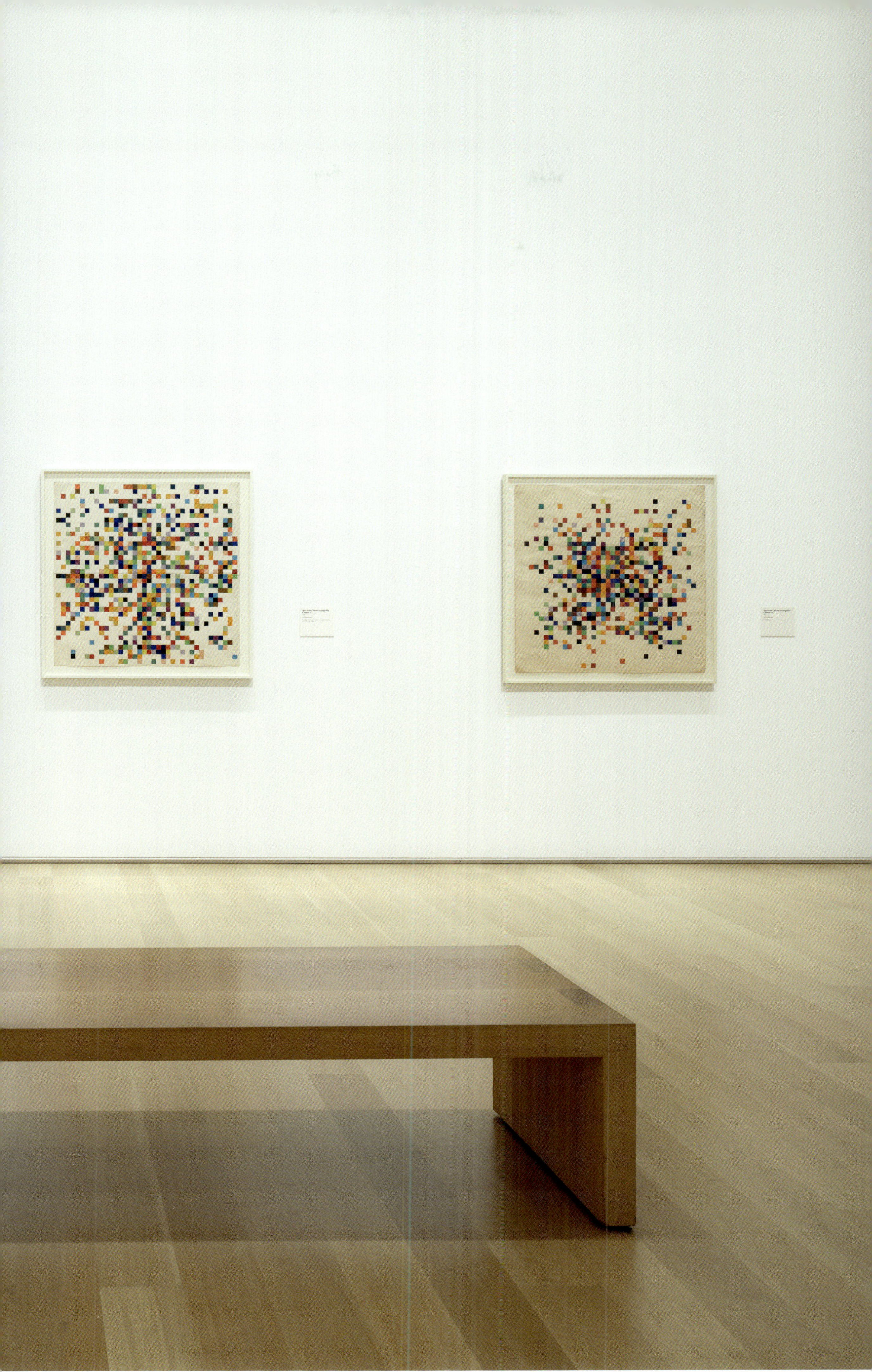

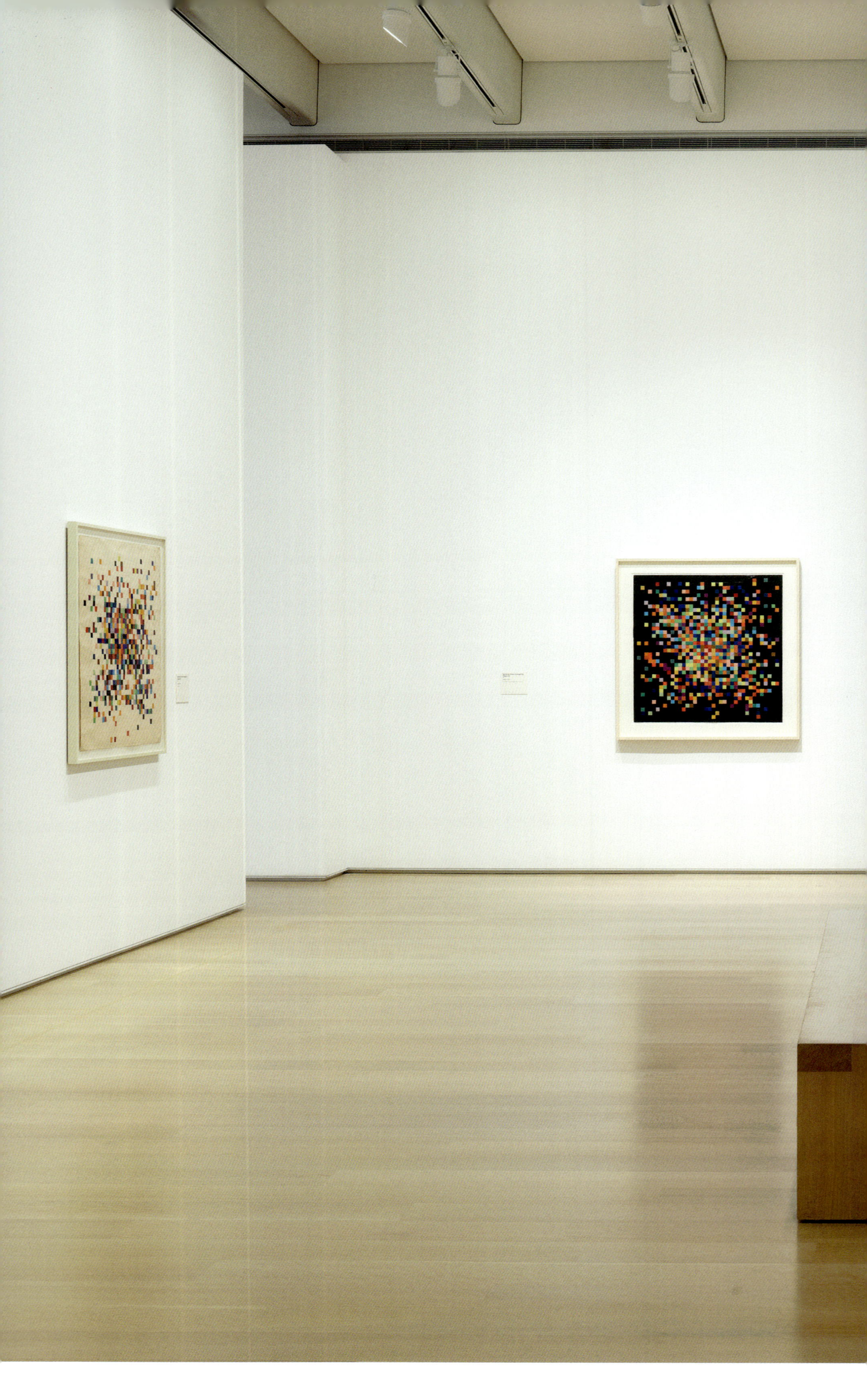

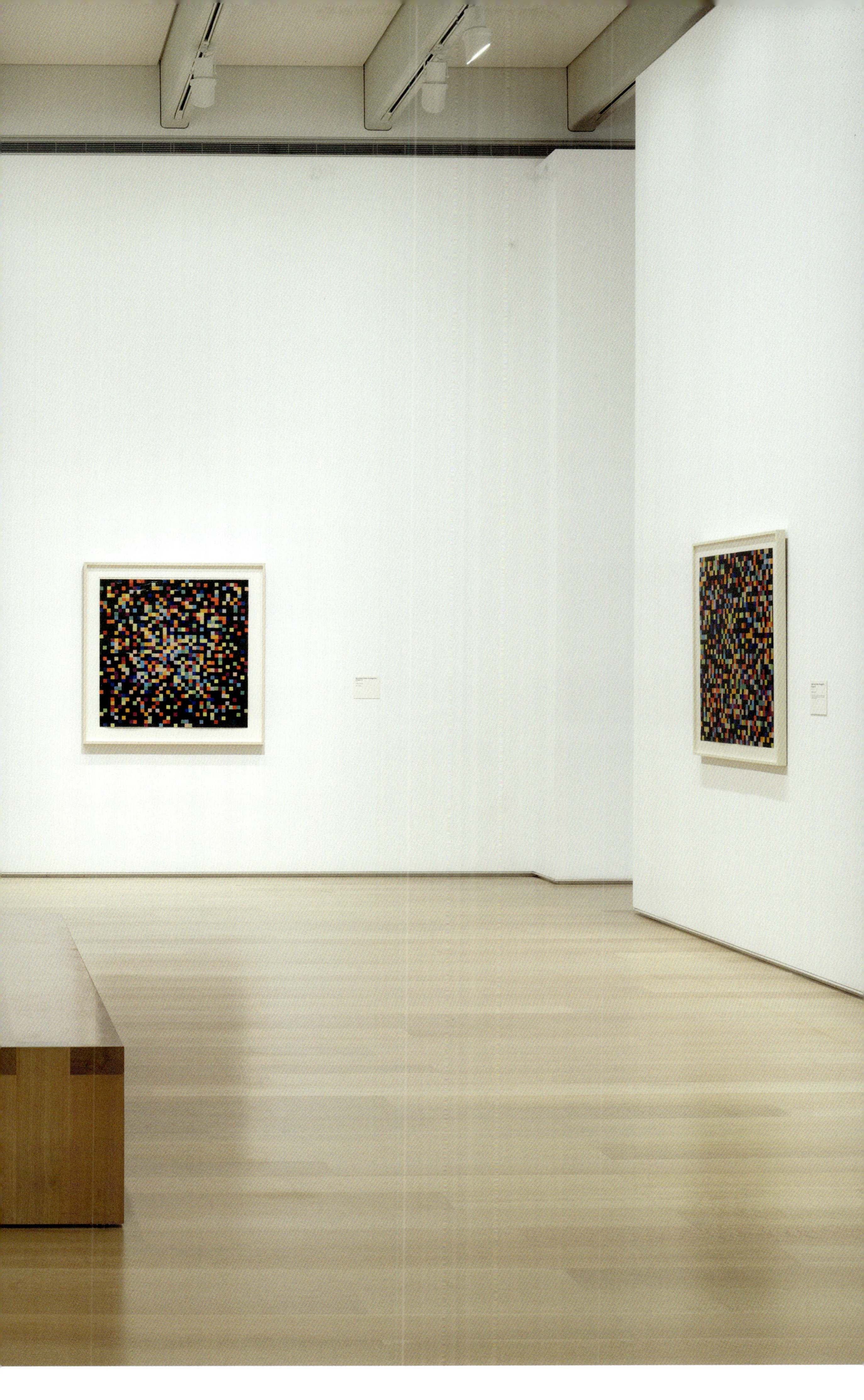

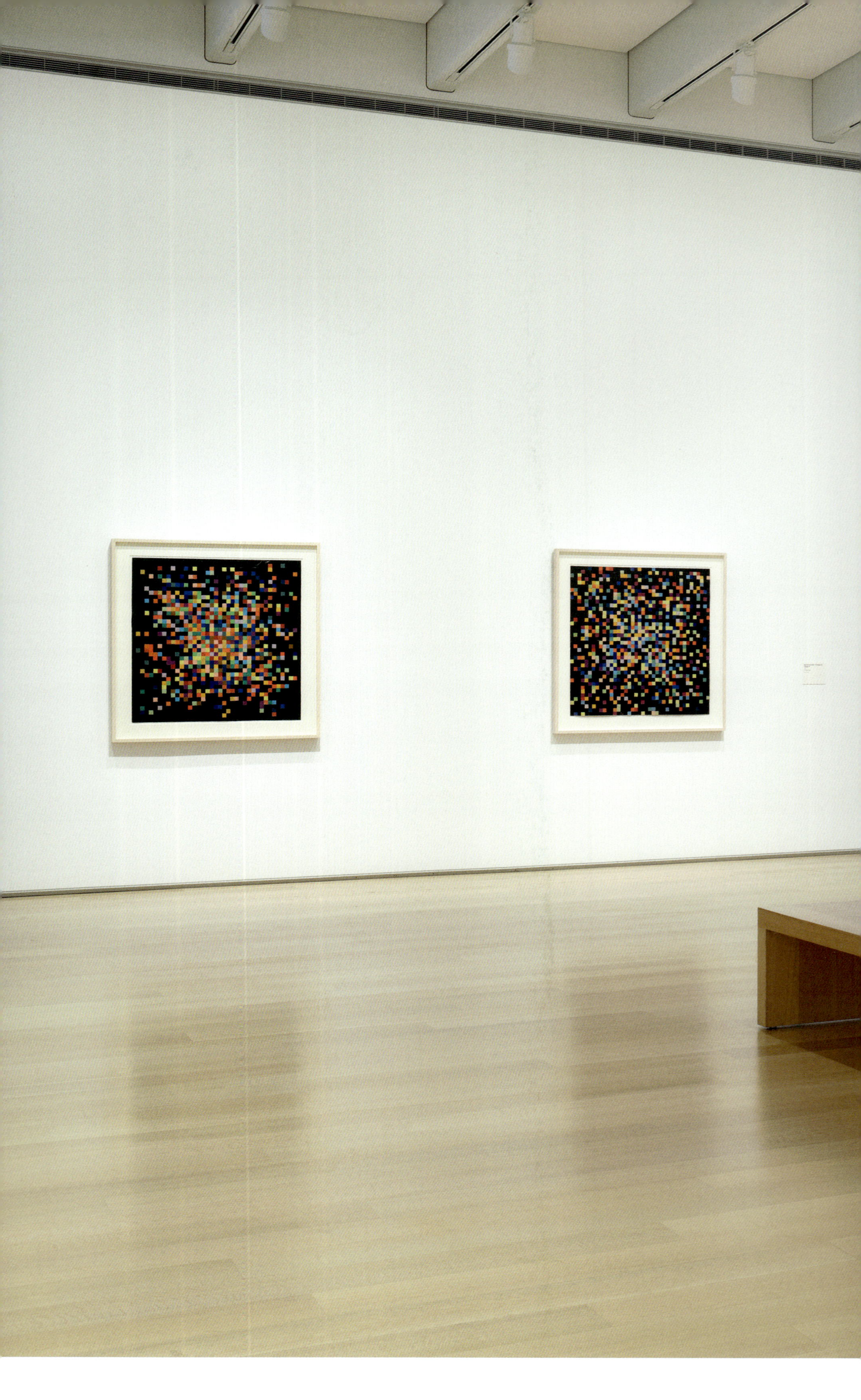

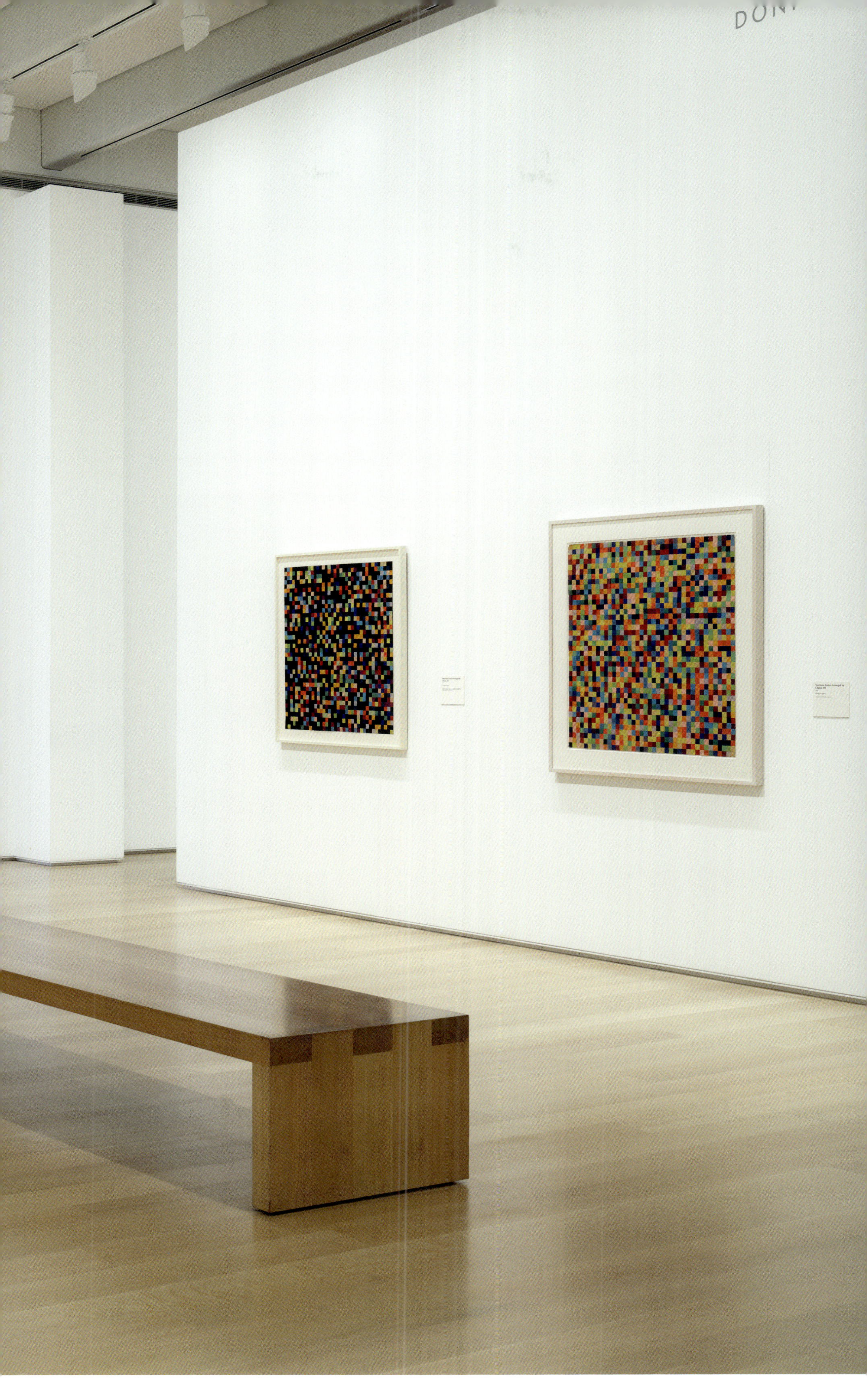

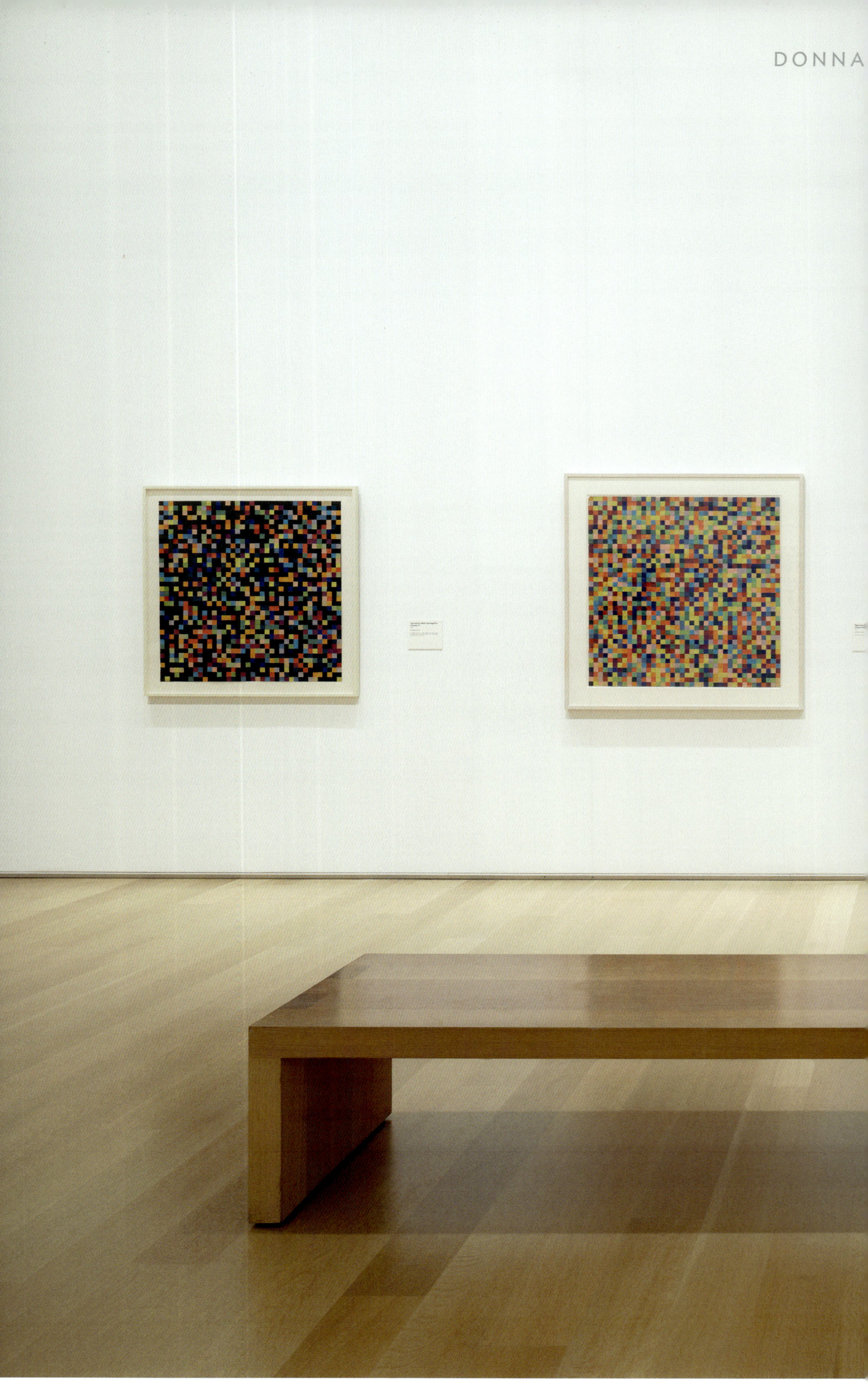

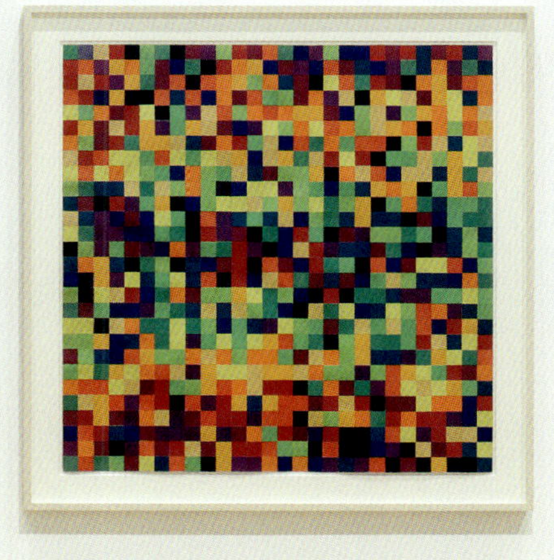
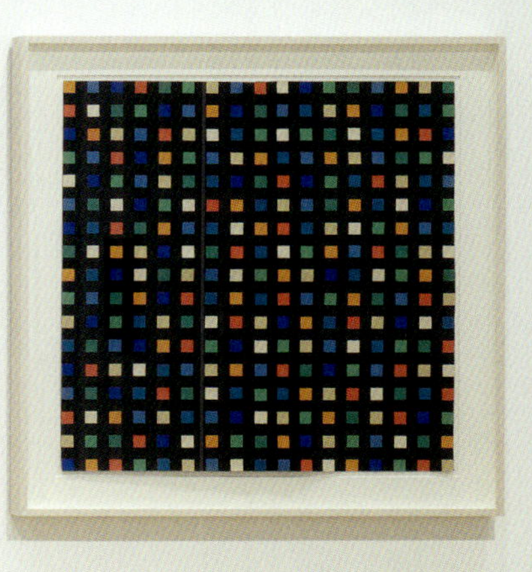
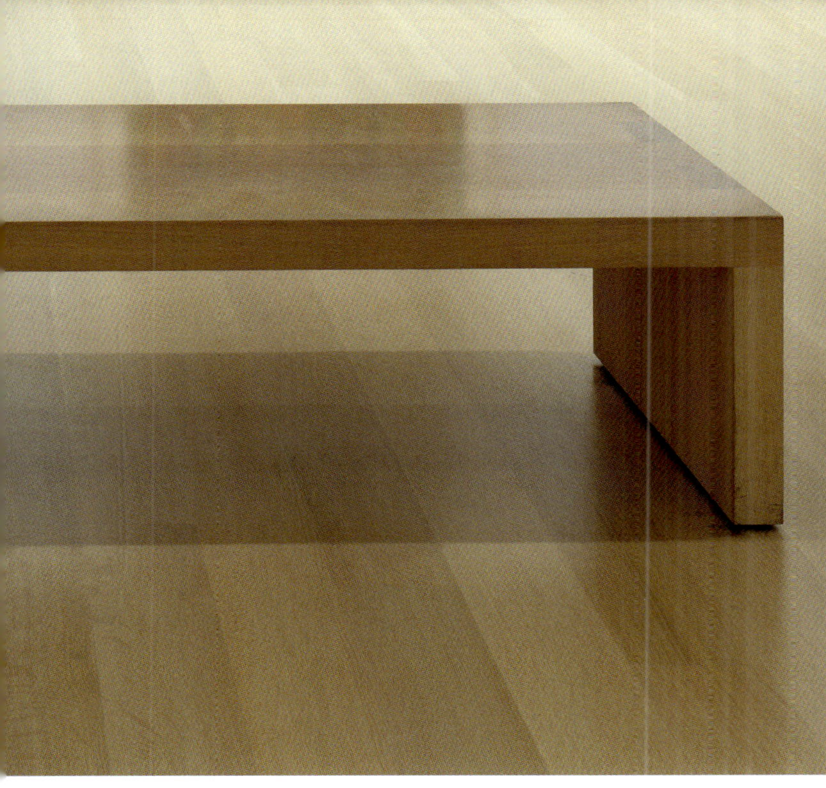

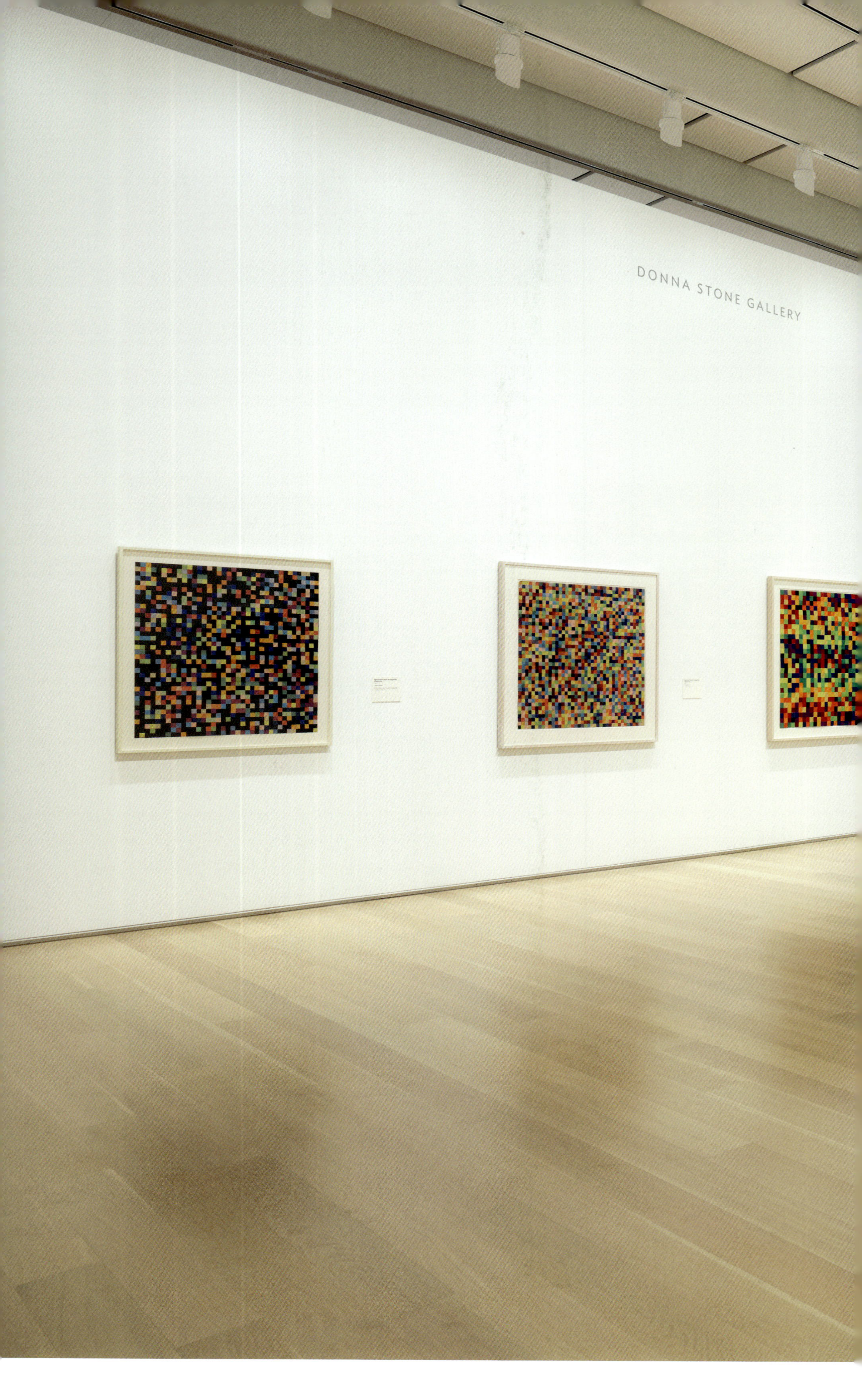
DONNA STONE GALLERY

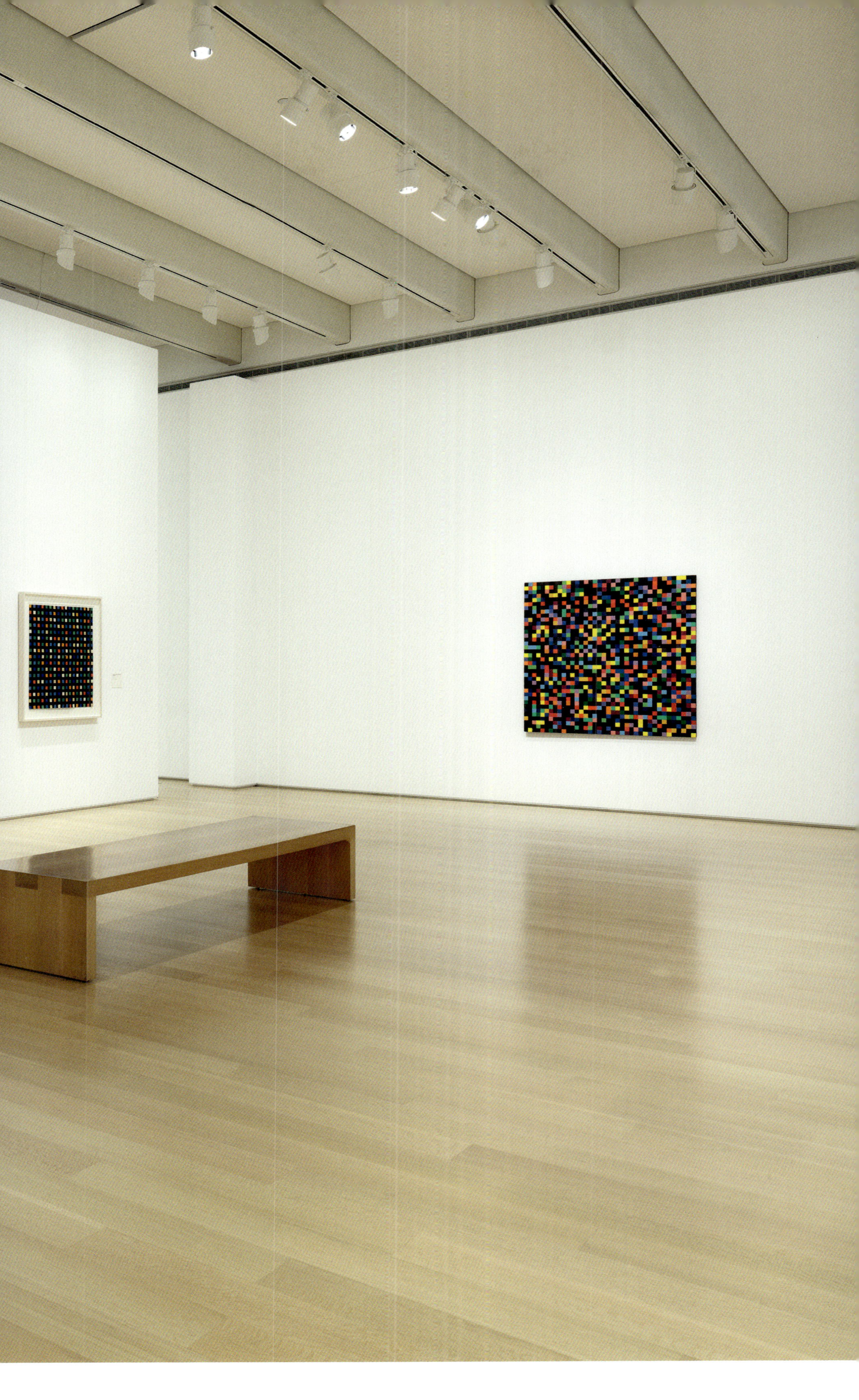

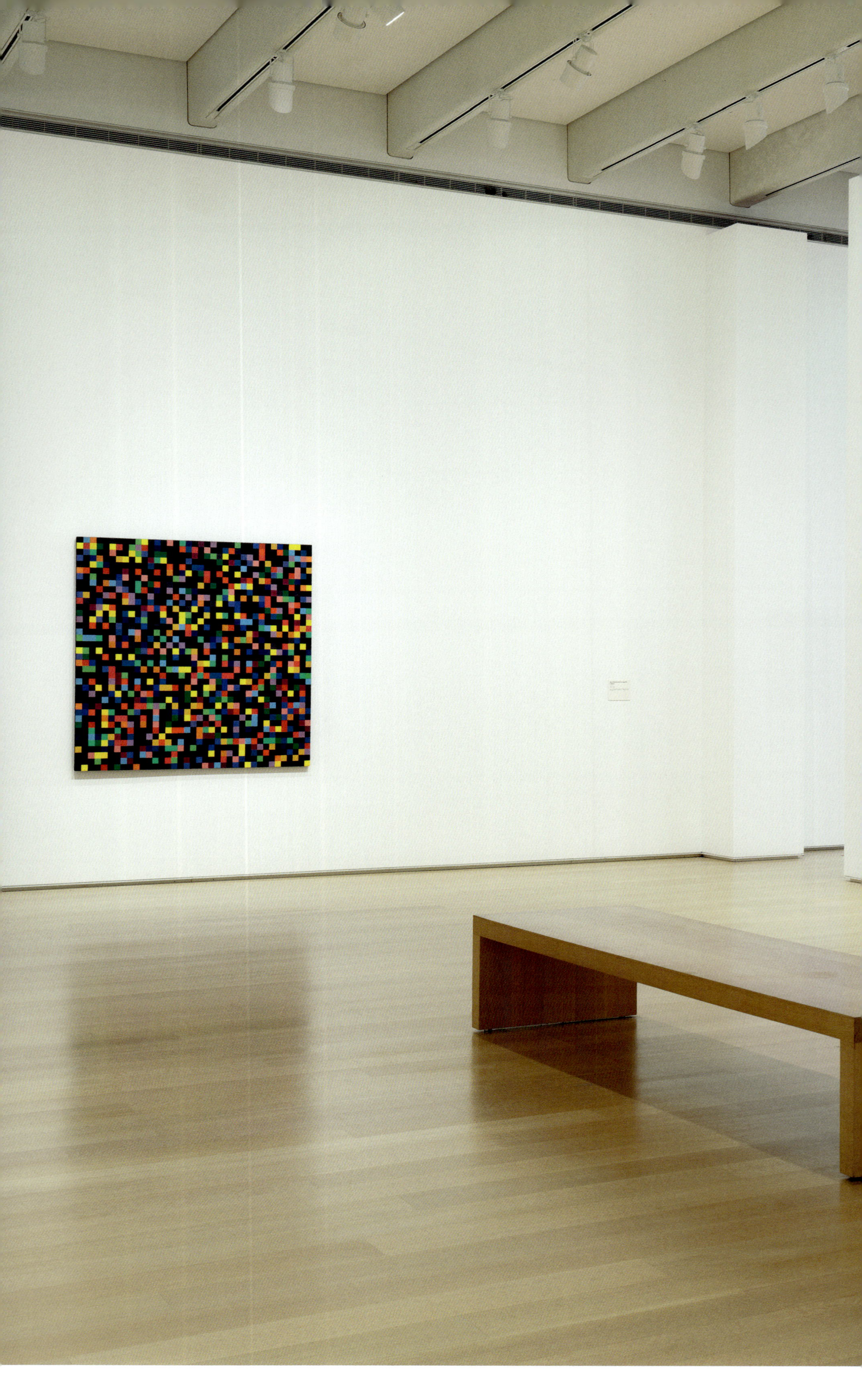

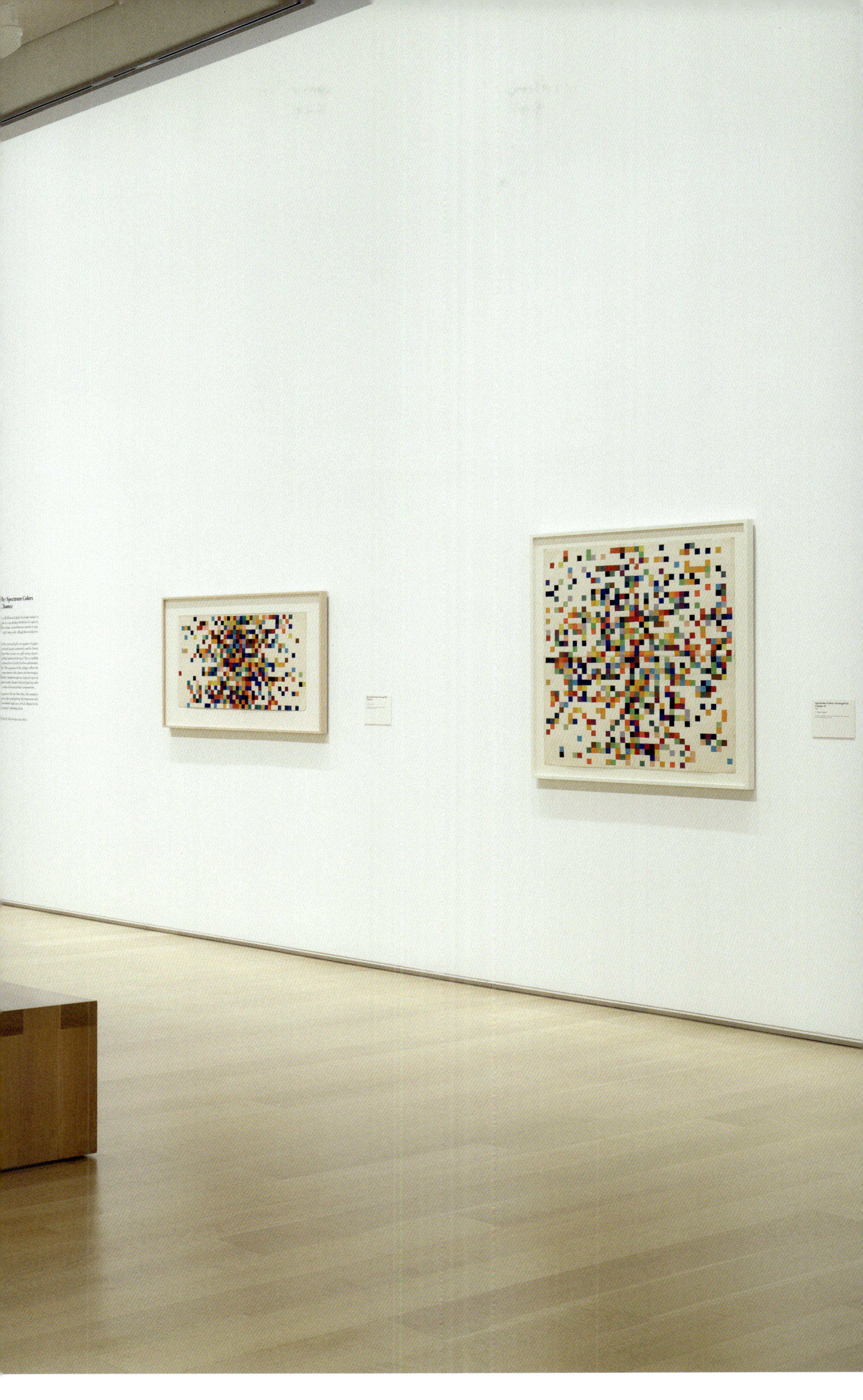